What Animals Can Teach Us about Spirituality

Inspiring Lessons from Wild and Tame Creatures

Diana L. Guerrero

Walking Together, Finding the Way
SKYLIGHT PATHS Publishing
Woodstock, Vermont

What Animals Can Teach Us about Spirituality:
Inspiring Lessons from Wild and Tame Creatures

2003 First Printing
© 2003 by Diana L. Guerrero

Library of Congress Cataloging-in-Publication Data

Guerrero, Diana L.
What animals can teach us about spirituality : inspiring lessons from wild and tame creatures / Diana L. Guerrero.
p. cm.
Includes bibliographical references.
ISBN 1-893361-84-5 (pbk.)
1. Animals—Religious aspects. 2. Human-animal relationships—Religious aspects. 3. Spiritual life. I. Title.
BL439 .G84 2003
204—dc22

2003013897

10 9 8 7 6 5 4 3 2 1
Manufactured in the United States of America
Interior art by Drena Fagen

SkyLight Paths Publishing is creating a place where people of different spiritual traditions come together for challenge and inspiration, a place where we can help each other understand the mystery that lies at the heart of our existence.

SkyLight Paths sees both believers and seekers as a community that increasingly transcends traditional boundaries of religion and denomination—people wanting to learn from each other, *walking together, finding the way.*

SkyLight Paths, "Walking Together, Finding the Way" and colophon are trademarks of LongHill Partners, Inc. registered in the U.S. Patent and Trademark Office.

Walking Together, Finding the Way
Published by SkyLight Paths Publishing
A Division of LongHill Partners, Inc.
Sunset Farm Offices, Route 4, P.O. Box 237
Woodstock, VT 05091
Tel: (802) 457-4000   Fax: (802) 457-4004
www.skylightpaths.com

Dedicated to the memory of Clyde
and to all the spiritual animals.

"In the beginning of all things, wisdom and knowledge were with the animals, for Tirawa, the One Above, did not speak directly to man. He sent certain animals to tell man that he showed himself through the beasts, and that from them, and from the stars and the sun and the moon, man should learn."

Chief Letakots-Lesa of the Pawnees
to Natalie Curtis in *The Indians Book* (1907)

A Note from the Author

Historically, human-animal comparisons provided sources of moral instruction and examples. Within this book you'll find analogies tied to animal behavior. All creatures exhibit a wide range of "good" and "bad" traits. Anthropomorphizing is considered heresy in some circles, but people remember animal examples and stories. So, I have taken creative license and described them from my human perspective. In this work, all stories, people, and animals are real. With few exceptions, the names have been changed and the stories have been combined or altered to maintain anonymity.

Contents

Preface: Becoming a Spiritual Animal

"Fish." My grandfather and I giggled uncontrollably while each of us took turns trying to say the word clearly. As a Mexican immigrant, he spoke with a heavy accent, and I was an infant working on my first word. In the end, we were quite pleased with ourselves. Witnesses shook their heads, chuckling at the oddity of my first utterance, which proved to be a prophecy of my future.

Although animals lived in my home as I grew up in California, my childhood asthma prevented my parents from keeping them. Instead, I made do with a large menagerie of stuffed animals. Deemed a dusty hazard to my health, these plush pals were eventually ripped from my clutches, too.

Despite those early challenges, animal friends always found their way into my life. Wild animals visited our yard, I watched the birds of prey soaring above the nearby fields, the neighborhood pets joined me on walks, and I covertly cared for the wayward animals who managed to find their way to our doorstep. Somehow animals always surrounded me.

My two loves are animals and the ocean, so when it came to considering a vocation, a career in the marine world seemed logical. My first declaration to the universe as an infant manifested at the ripe old age of fifteen when I began work as a volunteer marine naturalist and a narrator for whale watch tours.

To say I was driven is an understatement. If not out surfing at dawn, I could be found on the docks, waiting to embark on a whale watch vessel with hordes of school children, or perched on the rocky crags of the tide pools. Evenings were no different. I loved being on the sea under the stars as we sailed to Catalina Island, or on the shore leading onlookers to the grunion glimmering in the moonlight.

In addition to practical experience, I obtained academic training and special certifications along the way. My path meandered as I moved from the natural environment to a marine park, followed by a jaunt into the world of terrestrial animals. My work with land animals took me into captive wildlife handling and training for the entertainment industry. Some of my best teachers were the creatures most people call animal actors.

Lions, tigers, bears, elephants, snakes, and chimpanzees filled my days and tore me away from my cliff-dwelling existence into a hot and smoggy environment. Despite the glamour most people imagine when they think of the movie and television industry, I found the days on the sets long and boring. My happiest moments consisted of working with animals at the ranch, prepping them for their camera appearances. Captivated by the individuality of each animal and by the differences among species, I thirsted for knowledge, which motivated me to pursue a broader perspective. Soon I found myself entering the zoological realm.

At that time, only two animal training colleges existed. The first focused on training animal actors for Hollywood, while the second involved zoological institutions and marine parks. Facing tough competition, I vied against other candidates for one of the coveted spots. I found myself in a zookeepers' boot camp where I was required to maintain an acceptable grade point average while I also slaved away at tasks related to animal care. Those responsibilities included zoo-keeping; training animals; participating in internships at other facilities; patrolling the premises during night watch duties; and other assorted tasks, such as performing shows with live animals for audiences that ranged from a small handful of people to hundreds of onlookers.

If those duties were not enough, I traveled to other animal institutions, where I inspected every detail related to animal care and facility design, and explored every department and exhibit allowed. I pestered and picked the brains of anyone involved with animals to glean hidden insights from their experiences and personal knowledge. I visited small and large animal institutions throughout the United States, attended professional conferences, and explored anything else animal-related in the process. Sometimes my experiences were a bit awe inspiring.

For instance, when I met my first killer whale, she asked me to rub her tongue by coming up to me on the platform and opening her mouth full of very large conical teeth. As she bobbed up and down in front of me, I took a deep breath and stuck my hand past those daggers to rub her tongue. It took a whole lot of trust to oblige such a request.

Eventually, I traveled to the United Kingdom and Europe to train and work in conservation. There I learned about the complex challenges related to such tasks, and I worked with people from all over the world and with animals so endangered that fewer than a dozen existed in the wild. Most of those critters originated from small exotic places hard to locate unless you owned a special map. A few of the more obscure creatures I encountered included the volcano rabbit, the pink pigeon, and the round island gecko.

Because my nontraditional career includes a wide variety of experiences and roles, it is difficult to summarize. I've worked with animal welfare groups, in animal shelters, at animal rescue leagues, on the forefront of the animal disaster realm, at veterinary clinics, with zoo veterinarians, at pet and feed stores, on ranches, in private and public zoos, and with municipal agency animal programs. I've conducted seminars about animals and their behavior; taught pet owners how to deal with their animal delinquents; helped zookeepers overcome animal problems; and appeared on television, on radio, and in other media.

When I literally "fell" into writing after a tumble from the top of a zoo hay barn left me unable to perform my normal duties, I didn't imagine where the path might lead. I just followed it. The fall also thrust me into the exploration of alternative healing modalities and spiritual practices, and I became an affiliate of a progressive animal clinic. Ultimately, a series of synchronistic events led me to write this book.

I've walked in many moccasins on a road where trail tangents led to interesting insights and knowledge. The journey has finally brought me to a place where I have the opportunity to share the insights gleaned from my lifetime with animals. I'd like to connect people to animals so that they can understand and care for them, but there is more to it.

Animals remain bound to Spirit and do not follow any religion or spiritual practices. Because of that direct connection many of us lack, animals can link us to the Divine in new ways. In essence, animals can help us in our personal and spiritual growth, and compel us to pursue a connection to Spirit without the need for a religious or denominational approach. Some people search their entire lives for such a connection. Learning how to relate to animals can be a first step to recognizing how to unite with your spirit. This book will help.

Introduction: Following Animal Tracks to Spirituality

A nimals serve as a link to the intuitive and to the Divine. You cannot be around animals for any amount of time and not learn
something. For me, this means hidden lessons beyond the pragmatic
training relationships and application of behavioral theories.

In this book, I will present methods and examples designed to give
you a better understanding of animals; knowledge necessary to achieve
clear communication and establish mutual respect; and illustrations of
how animals help us tap into our spiritual natures and catalyze personal growth. Each level of growth ties into all the others, for we are a complete unit, not segments.

Spiritual maturation throughout life can be like climbing a spiritual ladder. Every rung contains specific lessons, and as you complete
each module, you step up to the next level. However, you might go up
and down the ladder multiple times. The same is true of personal
growth; sometimes we repeat lessons until we get them.

In organizing this book, I designed the first seven chapters to represent seven archetypal rungs. The first rung includes basic survival
beliefs, and the rungs ascend to the acts of faith, prayer, and meditative
thought patterns that compose the seventh.

The chapters introduce you to the feathered, finned, scaled, and furred creatures who served as my students and teachers. Each section incorporates more animals than the one whose name graces the chapter title. "Loyalty of the Dog" introduces us not only to dogs, but also to elephants, a sea lion, musk oxen, and some fabulous felines. In discussions about relationships, I relate stories that reflect themes of responsibility, balance, fairness, integrity, power, loyalty, honor, and justice.

"Playfulness of the Otter" illustrates the importance of hard work, relaxation, and play. In addition to taking a close look at our rapport with others, this chapter explores the inner child, physical desires, and persistence. We'll look at control, judgments, emotions, creativity, and the energy behind choices, guided by a menagerie of canines, marine mammals, a horse, and a cat.

"Power of the Polar Bear" seduces us into the world of physical power and emotional strength and impels us to investigate intuition, empowerment, self-acceptance, and confidence. Bears, cats, insects, and coyotes escort us.

"Heart of the Lion" helps us delve into compassion and love, while reminding us to focus on our relationships and urging us to face our adversaries. You'll meet TJ the mongrel and glimpse the world of animal rescue and dog training.

"Call of the Wolf" is purely a canine discourse, where wolves and domestic dogs lead the way through surrender, confession, acceptance, listening, and tuning into nature.

"Vision of the Eagle" helps us look at far-sightedness, inner vision, detachment, discernment, mindfulness, and letting go. Eagles, pelicans, bats, and bears serve as our instructors.

"Mind of the Dolphin" encourages us to probe the topics of harmony, synchronicity, and the importance of breathing. Our conductors include both domestic and wild animals.

The eighth chapter plays a different role from those of the first seven. "Wisdom of the Owl" includes practical instruction on how to develop your skills to connect with animals and, ultimately, with the Divine.

Finally, the Afterword is designed to stimulate your thoughts about animals in the afterlife. "Creatures of the Divine" briefly examines the question of animal souls. Join me on this quest and discover what animals can teach us about spirituality.

1

Loyalty of the Dog

Reina's puppies were everywhere. Less than twenty-four hours old, the pups were concerned with keeping warm, finding a meal, and recharging through sleep. Reina's only concerns were keeping her pups safe, fed, and clean. She responded quickly to their calls by nuzzling them closer to her body and up to her teats. The puppies emitted little grunting noises and whines as they rooted around searching for a connection. Once established, they became quiet and relaxed. Quite simply, this is how we all start on our journey up the spiritual ladder. We seek a connection.

As companions to humans for thousands of years, dogs have served as fellow hunters, loyal protectors, beloved family members, and constant companions. Like most animals, dogs embody ideal traits, serve as good examples of right action, and teach us many other lessons. Loyalty is one of those ideal traits.

Like the puppies, we first root around searching for answers to our immediate needs, however basic. Next we step out with the support of our closest relatives and friends, and finally we venture out into the world to make it as independent beings. Physical and social yearnings give way to spiritual longings and exploration.

Some people satiate that craving and find solace in nature, while others find it in a synagogue, chapel, cathedral, mosque, zendo, or temple. Some individuals experience the quest as a conscious journey and go as willing participants; others kick and resist until some event, or catalyst, thrusts them into a spiritual crisis.

A spiritual quest or crisis often places us at the base of the spiritual ladder. When we step onto the first rung, the desire is to just fit in. Many individuals, animal and human, strive for group recognition or to develop power and authority. At this level, we are concerned with basic survival necessities: nourishment, hydration, physical wellness, and safety. In relation to animals, these needs involve us as caretakers, teachers, and nurturers.

As companions to humans for thousands of years, dogs have served as fellow hunters, loyal protectors, beloved family members, and constant companions. Pack animals by nature, dogs live a shorter life than we do. We watch them grow, enter into a new family (humans), survive the trials of adolescence, mate and rear pups, mellow as they mature, and finally pass to another realm. With luck, a number of these companions accompany us through our lives at one time or another. Like most animals, dogs, during their condensed life, embody ideal traits, serve as good examples of right action, and teach us many other lessons. Loyalty is one of those ideal traits.

Bringing Out the Best in Each Other

William, a homeless man, arrived at McDonald's to get his morning meal. Outside, on a blanket next to his bicycle, was his dog. An American Staffordshire mix, the dog was in good physical shape and was a healthy weight. As William returned to share his breakfast with his companion, the loyalty between them showed, and the mutual love shone brightly through their eyes. I asked William about his life and current predicament. The encounter impressed me, because his relationship with his dog helped William be a better man despite his situation.

William took odd jobs for food and sometimes for money. This particular McDonald's fed him in exchange for his help maintaining the outside area of the restaurant. Both William and his dog slept out under the stars each night because William hated the attitudes of many of the homeless shelter helpers, the threat of theft, and the policy of "no pets allowed." The dog kept vagrants at bay. Inseparable, the two felt at home with the coyotes in the fields and the stars in the sky as their companions.

William kept on the straight and narrow because of the dog. The canine growled and barked in protest if William acted inappropriately. To prove his point, William got up and lunged toward me; the dog quickly stepped between us and barked at him. As William reassured the dog, he smiled at me. William is loyal and gives the dog his best. The animal is devoted to his human, comforts him, and protects him. The dog also alerts William to what behavior is acceptable and what is not.

Animals make us want to be better people. Humans go to great lengths to help animals and small children. I wonder how many folks open up to William because of the loyalty and love of his canine companion. The duo exemplifies interdependence, how two beings support one another to achieve balance no matter what the outside circumstances may be. Canine protectiveness is motivated by love and concern, and the dog's display of loyalty is a good example for humans to note.

In humans, motivation rooted in loyalty and love can lead to change. In other cases, it can result in taking a stand over concerns for the welfare of another. Animal stewardship is an important responsibility. As we bulldoze land and build human communities, we destroy many animal habitats. As a result, animal populations dwindle. The fate of many creatures remains in our hands through zoological facilities or similar organizations.

Threats to human or animal life trigger lessons related to personal influence, integrity, responsibility, and sometimes a fight against the tribal status quo. Tribal behavior requires members to stick together. In the past, this related to survival. Today, this is not the case. However, gang members, athletic teams, and unions illustrate contemporary examples of clannish conduct. A human who goes against the majority takes a risk.

Going against the grain can lead to confrontation, aggression, and unpopularity. As a surrogate parent to animals, I get very protective over my charges. In one case, it tested my convictions and my endurance.

Choosing a Life of Integrity

As I tromped through the underbrush with my canine companion, I quizzed the heavens. "Why me? Why am I the one who always has to be accountable?" The answer echoed in my head, "To whom much is given, much is required." I bellowed, "That is not the answer I wanted!" But I knew deep in my soul it was true.

This particular incident involved a large group of zoo elephants. The caretakers hated the management and the management distrusted the handlers; the environment was hostile. Public outcry over dangerous elephant incidents had pushed everyone into a corner. In the animal training world, frustration, fear, or distrust usually breeds aggression. In this case, the aggression escalated in both the animals and the humans.

As I watched the ebb and flow of power struggles, dishonesty, and passive-aggressive behavior in the humans involved, my concerns grew. Although wild animals act aggressively when necessary, it is not usually their first choice. As the elephant aggression increased, my blood turned cold. I witnessed an incident where an elephant stalked one of her keepers. It is a bad omen when a herbivore, an animal who doesn't hunt, pursues a human. Unwittingly, I had found a big can of worms and jumped in with both feet.

Ultimately, I chose to take action, because, at the very least, it would make my coworkers safe and improve conditions for the animals. It was a grueling process. I attempted to catalyze change from within, but it didn't work. Eventually, I pursued legal avenues, to no avail. I moved on with my life in the belief that I had lost the battle, but I was wrong.

After I left, changes took place in the elephant department. The despised managers and supervisor moved to a different facility, the zoo purchased new equipment, and open discussions without the fear of repercussion occurred during meetings. On a return visit, two and a half years later, I heard, "You really have no idea how much change you created." When I saw the elephants, my spirit reconnected.

As I entered the inner sanctum behind the show arena, the girls rushed to greet me. They rumbled and moved in close, touching me with their trunks, breathing in my scent, and asking me to breathe into their trunks. Sidra turned and leaned in closely, blocking Deirdre. Reaching over the barriers, Deirdre opened her mouth. Both elephants wanted me to rub their tongues, which is an intimate elephant greeting.

Their ears flapped in excitement, and they moved their trunks over my mouth and all around me to make sure it was me. I kept rubbing their rough bodies, breathing in their scent, and blowing into their trunks. I rubbed Sidra's tongue, and she rumbled and trumpeted. They kept sliming me with their snotty trunks. There is nothing like an unfettered display of pachyderm affection.

The elephants had motivated me to define my priorities and take a stand. I could either "sell my soul" or "make a statement to the universe." So, I chose to do the right thing no matter what the cost. Animals were the catalysts for my motivation and my actions.

My lesson involved a test of personal integrity, taking personal responsibility, and using personal influence to create change. It required that I become conscious about issues of importance on a deeper level and about my relationship to the larger plane of the world.

Shortly after my affirming visit with the elephants, one of my favorite ministers, Wendy Craig-Purcell, challenged her congregation to examine their behavioral choices when they were alone. Wendy asked: How do you behave when nobody is looking? If the light is red and nobody is around, do you go through? Do you keep the wrong change if it is wrong in your favor? What if an instant teller dispenses a few extra hundred dollars that does not show on your withdrawal slip, what then? Do you decide to tell a white lie to save face, to avoid something? Do you park in a no-parking zone? Your true self is revealed by what you do when nobody is looking. Animals pass the test with flying colors.

Animals are the same no matter what. A dog telegraphs clearly whether it likes you or hates you. Perhaps you have come home to a dog who has done something wrong. Does he hide from you? Usually the answer is *no*. The dog lowers his body and submits himself to your will. He takes responsibility and owns up to the crime. What is your reaction? If you are like me, you hunt around to find out what the confession is about. Your reaction is important. Honesty should not be punished.

The responsibility that comes with stewardship, power, or position is a big one. It requires integrity to be truthful and to do the right thing no matter who is looking or what the cost. When committed to a spiritual path, you do what is required to live up to your responsibility. The passage can be a difficult one. When balance is lost on this rung, it can result in some heartbreaking conditions, and it is usually the animals who suffer. In many cases, the imbalance is exhibited by trying to control or dominate.

Stewardship Is Not Domination

When the animal control officer and I arrived to inspect the state of affairs, my heart sank at the condition of the lion. Tethered on a chain out in the small backyard of a home on the outskirts of Los Angeles, the lion was malnourished and suffered from rickets. His skeletal structure could not support his weight, so he could not stand for any length of time or move without the risk of fracturing his bones. Instead of resembling a robust male complete with the signature mane, he looked like a lioness. Malnourishment and inadequate care prevented his proper development.

The distraught animal control officer shook his head while telling me the lion's owner insisted the large feline could be a vegetarian. Because of the owner's naïveté, the lion did not receive the proper diet. The man took the passage from the Book of Isaiah that says "And the lion shall eat straw like the ox" (Isaiah 11:7) literally. The owner believed the lion could survive by eating vegetation. Furthermore, the man expected the lion to then lie down peacefully with animals normally eaten by the beast. The poor creature could hardly move. The person was going to prove his point no matter what the cost.

Fortunately I did not meet the human responsible. Was he deranged, naïve, or power hungry? He exhibited a warped idea of domination, where control over another living being symbolizes great strength. He failed to meet his obligation as a steward to the animal. Animals, especially wild ones, have unique needs far beyond domesticated creatures. Physical power or control is not inner strength. True power comes from a spiritual center, not a physical one.

This story illustrates the need for growth. It becomes visible in the animal realm when people do not provide basic care for their critters, when they abandon or relinquish their charges, or when they are just plain abusive. In group animal-training courses, imbalance is exhibited when owners bark orders or commands incessantly, physically try to force animals to do their will, or engage in dishonorable actions, such as pushing a pup's face into its own excrement (a common old-school dog training technique), thinking the action discourages future accidents. The method does not work, and there are other ways to teach proper behavior.

Animals simply accept their humans and what is dished out. In a balanced relationship, calmness prevails and animals depend fully on the human for all or most of their needs. Those truly in power do not assert it. Just watch animals competing for attention or with each other. They rely on subtle posturing to express their thoughts and feelings.

Dominant dogs do not always assert themselves. There is an acknowledged order and etiquette in the dog world. For example, Sam, a shepherd, was an assertive animal. He held his body and tail up high. When he met other dogs, he stood tall. He went through doors first, ate first, and greeted his owners first. When the pup Rusty arrived, it seemed as though Rusty did nothing but agitate Sam. The owners did not like when Sam growled and pinned him. However, Sam taught Rusty boundaries and etiquette. Because these dog owners knew enough to let the canines sort it out, nothing horrible happened. The entire family now spends time together at home and out in public without any disharmony.

Trouble starts when people get the wrong idea and try to interfere. When dog owners try to even out the playing field, they cause problems. For instance, as a dominant male, Sam should be greeted first. Ignoring Sam and giving Rusty preferential treatment, or pushing Sam away in order to greet Rusty first, would have resulted in some serious altercations. Some people don't think it is fair for one dog to get attention over another. Those people want animal equality. In reality, animals function within a pecking order. Being fair is one thing; being astute and aware of the order of things is another. Some humans have a tough time accepting the natural hierarchy of the animal world, just as many people have trouble accepting things in their own lives.

When individuals witness injustice, rising emotions can include revenge, victim mentality, bitterness, and disappointment. However, the only real justice is divine justice. Reaching a positive position on this matter requires a shift away from expectations of how things "should be." Accepting events and outcomes are additional opportunities for growth.

Living in the Now

Animals accept things for how they are. They live in the moment and adjust accordingly. They teach us how to be present, and they call us to attention when we get lost in unimportant details. There is a saying: The past is gone, the future has yet to arrive, but the time we are in is precious and lasts only a short time. The point is that this moment is the only moment, it is a gift, and that is why it is called the present. Animals live in the present at all times. Their attention is on you, the situation, or the enthralling object of their desire, fully and completely. People say, "Be here now," "Live mindfully," and other such expressions. Animals have been trying to get us to notice the same message for eons.

Chloe is a calico cat who lives with Freemont, a dog, and their owner, Lisa. Chloe picked Lisa when she visited an animal shelter. Lisa said, "She reached out and grabbed me with her paw and refused to be ignored. I spent time with her, and then brought my dog, Freemont, to meet her so we could see how everyone got along. She took it all in stride and came home with us. Now she has been here five years."

Lisa's life is a busy one, but she rushes home to her precious pets every night. Between Chloe's antics and walks with Freemont she is always occupied. Lisa explained, "They really mean a lot to me. When I get home they conduct a greeting party. Freemont wags his tail frantically, brings me his favorite toys so I can play with him, and Chloe wraps herself around my ankles and legs. No matter what they are doing, or what time it is when I arrive, they are enthusiastic and I am their total focus. If I am distracted and rushing around, they follow me and wait until I have the sense enough to greet them."

Demonstrating how important Lisa is to them, and worthy of their full attention, is not the only role they play in her life. When Lisa gets too lost in her work, Chloe terrorizes her. "I can work for hours on end and lose total track of time. Freemont comes and nudges me, or brings me his ball when he figures it is time for a break, but Chloe is the little tyrant. She walks over and lies on my keyboard or on the papers I am grading. If I am reading, she simply jumps up and gets onto the book. I always know when I overdo it because they remind me."

Lisa admits she sometimes makes them wait, and they do cut her some slack when she really needs it. They work at showing her what is important. How often do we get distracted by the mechanics of daily life instead of being involved with the living beings around us? Lisa's animals assert themselves but also accept when she does not immediately give in to their demands. More significant, they are examples of the give and take required in any relationship, including accepting the actions and requests of those dear to them.

When asked about their pets, people mention they feel accepted for who they are, for what they do, and for all their faults. In general, many people do not feel accepted or that they belong. Friends and relatives used to live close by and had time to nurture the children of the local community, but these beneficial connections are no longer available to many of us.

No longer do people grow up in the same home where their ancestors lived. In my hometown, I went to school with kids whose parents had attended school with mine. My entire family lived in one town, and we saw each other all the time. Not too long ago, families immigrated to the United States and put down roots. Entire families grew up knowing their grandparents, aunts, uncles, and cousins because they saw them all the time. Neighbors knew each other and the families of those living close by. People felt accepted and part of a larger community. In all these situations, most people knew the pets in the neighborhood.

Why does everyone know the neighborhood pets? Animals illustrate unconditional acceptance. If you doubt this, go to a public place and observe a group of dogs running around. If you walk into an area of gregarious mutts, they run up to say hello, even if only briefly. If a group of dogs are playing and another strange dog approaches, every dog runs up to greet it. After the ritual "hellos" that include sniffing and posturing, the new animal can join in the antics. The well-socialized canine is a genial beast and each newcomer is welcomed without reservation. If the newcomer is not friendly, the situation usually diffuses quickly and the animal is left alone to her own devices. Whatever the expression, it is honest, direct, and accepted.

Animals don't just greet animals, but humans, too. Sparked by the desire for public interactions for their pets, people take their critters out for social interludes. Animals generate communities by bringing people together and motivating them to get to know one another.

Moving beyond Fear

Animals express themselves with honesty and integrity. For instance, if an animal is afraid or aggressive, she clearly shows it through her behavior, posture, and vocalizations.

Sadie was a timid German shepherd. Although many folks automatically thought she was abused as a young pup, this was not true. She simply was born with a submissive temperament.

There is a short window of time during puppyhood when dogs must learn proper social etiquette. If they do not, then the lack of socialization can make them predisposed to certain behavior problems, such as fear aggression. Sadie did not receive the needed socialization during the critical timeframe. Further complications included improper integration into her new home and harsh training methods, which contributed to her fear. She attacked when cornered or threatened.

Attacking was never her first choice. When she felt threatened, she growled, tucked her tail between her legs, and pulled down her ears. As a last resort to defend herself, Sadie backed up against her owner or wedged herself into a protected area. The same person might approach her at another time, in another environment, with no negative response. Sadie reacted to the circumstances of the moment.

The same goes for other behaviors. If an animal is aggressive, for instance, she telegraphs the warning in advance. If the warning is ignored, then consequences follow. We humans do not always pay attention to communication through vocalization, body language, and other subtle signals.

Animals such as Sadie can improve if the owners work diligently and adapt their lives to providing a secure and safe environment for the animal. Often, additional intervention beyond simple dog training is needed. Behavior modification, alternative therapies, and even pharmaceutical intervention can help severe cases. Sadie's owners believed her psyche was too delicate, the time commitment for change too much, and the risk to others too high. They opted for euthanasia. Sometimes putting an animal down is the most humane action.

The Fear Response

Wild animals have fears related to survival. A predator or unfamiliar creature causes intense observation in some species and flight in others. Instincts ensure their survival. However, there are times when some animals can gaze upon a predator and not stir. This is because they are so attuned to others that they sense when there is danger and when there isn't. Humans tend to lump all fears, realistic or irrational, together in one category requiring an emotional response. Part of our journey toward spiritual maturity is learning to distinguish between them and define the appropriate response.

Being aware of both intuitive and physically telegraphed messages has kept me safe with animals all these years. In some cases, I have refused to work with an animal based on a gut feeling and at other times based on signals I received from the animal. One such situation involved a bobcat.

When I approached the bobcat area of a small zoo, the animal was perched on top of her den box near the door to her enclosure. New to the facility, I had someone with me to supervise. The overseer asked me to enter the cage, but when I looked at the situation I knew it would be trouble. If I entered the cage, the cat perched above my body could easily leap onto my head, neck, or shoulders. The cat's eyes were fully dilated and her ears were cocked back in a manner indicating irritation. This information told me it was foolish to enter the exhibit unless the dynamics changed. Our options were to get her to shift her location or to address the chore at another time.

We discussed the matter and ultimately decided to entice the cat to move to another area. We could have forced her, but it is better to allow the animal a choice. Our simple action, calling her to the other side of the exhibit for a reward, changed her mood and distracted her. Once she was comfortable in another area of the pen, our task was completed with ease.

Sometimes we miss the signals humans or animals send. Density, or inattentiveness, gets us into uncomfortable situations. If one person involved in an altercation is fearful or hostile, then it is best to take a step back. Taking the time to assess the situation reveals when it is best to deal with problems head on and when it is best to leave them until a later time. Force or arguments seem to accomplish nothing more than to create defensiveness, hostility, or resentment. Shifting the situation, coming back to it, or allowing a safe retreat for the other individual are better strategies. They are also the same strategies used with animals.

Most animals avoid altercations if they can. It is risky to their survival and health. If two domestic cats are at odds, they posture and emit verbal warnings. Then they either agree on a draw and move away from each other or enter into a fight. The consequences of fighting are serious, so skirmishes don't happen too often. The consequences humans face are miserable too, because nothing positive usually results from altercations.

All of the animal species of this world have a specific function. They are uniquely adapted to life in their particular environments and have jobs that keep nature in balance. When left alone, they live in a harmony that keeps the environment equalized. Our species tends to be disruptive, trying to improve on what is already working. In the process, we domesticated animals and molded them for a life with humans. Some of these animals can develop phobias. It is rare for a captive wild animal to have irrational fears, but some do.

Kelpie the sea lion's phobia involved any man wearing a cowboy hat and sunglasses. When we came out onto the stage she could pick out a man outfitted with the dreaded garb in the middle of a hundred people. Her fears may have been rooted in a memory of a prior experience with a trainer who liked to wear those accessories, or it could have been some weird quirk. If I did not spot the innocent offender first and adjust the situation, she bolted off stage. Sometimes an assistant asked the man to remove the offending items, or I distracted Kelpie with a complex routine. If I failed to keep her occupied or comfortable while the dreaded hat and glasses were present, she bolted.

People exhibit similar idiosyncrasies, and animals trigger many human fears. When I first started doing animal shows, the biggest satisfaction for me was turning the gasps of horror and squeals of fear into ones of wonder and respect. The animals who generated these intense reactions were always the reptiles, especially snakes and tarantulas, as well as unfamiliar animals, such as vultures.

Spiders and snakes are the most common animals people fear. There is a primal reaction to these creatures that borders on panic. In reality, these animals are fascinating and not as dangerous as a tiger or a chimpanzee. Although innumerable people express the desire to pet a tiger or play with an ape or monkey, the reality is those animals are more likely to maim and hurt a person. The smaller nonvenomous spider or sleek snake can't hurt most people because their mouths are too tiny. However, these phobias are so common that they even have specific names: arachnophobia for spiders and ophidiophobia for snakes.

Helping One Another

A musk ox is a shaggy-coated animal with horns that form a shield and serve as a helmet on the crest of the skull. The horns follow the profile close to the sides of the head and then curve up like sharp hooks. These animals have a strategy to protect the vulnerable members of their herd and thwart predators, such as wolves and bears. The adults use their bodies to form a fortress, keeping the calves in the center. The cows and bulls stand with their rumps on the inner circle and face their foes. If necessary, the mature males actually dash from the group to attack the menace. They often throw the predator into the air with a quick blow from their horns and deliver crushing strikes with their hooves. The musk ox is a good symbol of how to face your fears or take steps to alleviate them. Gather yourself together, confront what it is you need to deal with, use those gifts or tools you have to address the matter, and take action to resolve the situation.

Sometimes the issue seems bigger than it is, and when we face it, our perspective changes. If we consciously walk along the path of life, our opinions and perceptions change. One of my favorite animal illustrations is the change in society's viewpoint about wolves. At one time, wolves were plentiful in the United States and Europe. Although Native Americans have always honored wildlife, other settlers and cultures did not. Folklore and fairy tales painted wolves as savage, cunning, and bloodthirsty animals. Those views struck fear and hatred in the hearts of villages and settlements. Sadly, wolves were persecuted as savage beasts and hunted for their pelts to the brink of extinction.

Today the story is completely different. Through our steps to protect these animals, observations, interactions, and research studies reveal quite a different picture than what was painted in the past. Although wolves are known for having strong jaws and large teeth, they also are known for their prowess, family loyalty, tenderness with their pups, complex social groups, and patience with others in their pack. Wolves are now respected creatures who can teach us about family life and living in harmony with nature. The wolves have not changed, only our perspective.

Studying the lives of these canines hints at the things we can do to maintain a healthy family environment. Wolves show us that we should labor hard to work things out in our families; communicate on a constant basis; set fair and solid rules and abide by them; use kindness and firmness with our children; and use patience and understanding when dealing with others in intimate social groups and larger communities. We are lucky to have wolves in the wild and dogs in our homes.

Canines in our households give us unique opportunities to learn through their examples and struggles. At first puppies are timid and afraid to move away. They get lost. We watch those early beginnings, where the pups look for a connection, and notice that it does not last long. They soon begin to wander and explore. As we watch, the pups grow and move on to independence. They learn to recognize kindred spirits, their human caretakers, and their surroundings.

It isn't long before they romp, play, practice new skills, and develop into more independent critters. Just when it seems they are getting the hang of life, they are removed from their first family of canines into a home of humans. Once again, they are afraid. They cry, whimper, and look for comfort.

How is the pup to know that this is the same lesson again? This time the change includes learning to adapt to new surroundings. There are new relationships with strangers; some are human and some are animal. Now there are rules to be followed and a new language to learn. If left to her own devices, she gets into all kinds of mischief. Fortunately, the human home provides guidance and love. The pup strives to connect again. It is the connection and bond that takes the pup on a fresh journey. This journey is one of rebellion, maturation, and achievement.

When the pup achieves a sense of security, she strives to test the limits. These limits teach her what she can do and what she cannot. She expends lots of energy and becomes a source of laughter, frustration, and love. This phase brings laughter and light-heartedness to those within her home. And so we, too, move through our lessons, like the pup, onto the second rung of spiritual lessons.

2

Playfulness of
the Otter

The otters floated gently, lulled by the natural ebb and flow of the sea, embraced by the morning sun. The crash of the waves on the shore and the cry of the gulls were the only sounds on this pristine morning.

As I sipped my coffee, it struck me as odd that the otters should be so still. With intense metabolic needs, they are always on a quest for food. Their normal behavior is to dive over and over again for their fare. Surfacing shortly after, they float on their backs while snacking on sea urchins, mollusks, and crustaceans, often using a rock as a tool to break through shells to get at the nourishing flesh.

Otters remind us to be industrious and to work hard; to dive deep to get to the bottom of things; to be persistent to get what we need; to use innovation to break through barriers; and to make time to play and celebrate life.

When finished, they repeat the effort, or they begin an intense grooming session. Because otters lack a heavy blubber layer for warmth, they rely on the insulating properties of their pelts, which need constant cleaning and fluffing so the small air pockets formed in the process can provide further insulation. These critters are industrious, but if you were to watch them during a quiet moment such as this, you would never guess.

Although otters work hard, they also play hard. These skillful and agile swimmers pursue others, spin somersaults, chase their tails, or play hide and seek in the kelp. When cavorting swiftly through the water, their undulations can catapult them into the air and onto the rocky shore. Although they are mainly solitary, otters can form small groups and communities.

Otters remind us to be industrious and to work hard; to dive deep to get to the bottom of things; to be persistent to get what we need; to use innovation to break through barriers; and to make time to play and celebrate life. Many of us work long hours at our place of employment, labor at home on essential projects, toil in the yard, and slave away at work we bring home. Unfortunately, these tasks seem to take priority, and we forget to take time for ourselves and our families. We fail to play or celebrate small but significant events in our lives and those of our loved ones.

As I watched the otters relaxing, it reminded me of friends who practice prayer or meditation, who simply take the day off to honor the Sabbath or attend a retreat, or who spend a day writing poetry or practicing yoga. Striving to live in balance is essential to our spiritual development. We need time to recharge and appreciate all the aspects and activities of our lives. A holistic approach helps us accelerate our spiritual development.

The second stage of growth involves relationships with others, getting in touch with our inner child, physical desires, and work. Spiritual lessons at this rung of the ladder concern control, judgments, emotions, creativity, and the energy or intent behind choices.

Just as the otter needs to dive deep to get to the ocean floor, we need to get underneath the symptoms of any disharmony. Our descent to the bottom of our issues helps us purge any attachments to past patterns of behavior. Sometimes delving deep is scary, but animals motivate us to dive.

After starting to work with domestic animals and their owners, I began to notice two trends. First, people did not view their animals as individuals; instead, they projected their own issues and beliefs onto the animals and treated them as extensions of themselves. Second, the animals exhibited emotional or behavioral issues that were actually the humans' issues within the home. The animals mirrored behaviors for the household so the humans had a chance to view it from a distance or to deal with it indirectly.

For instance, a married couple in turmoil struggled for domination over each other. Their dog attempted to dominate them and refused to obey or cooperate with either person. In another case, a dog was hyperactive. When I arrived, I found the family in chaos. The dog became a common project, and the household environment calmed down during the training process. But behavioral and emotional concerns are not the only issues animals take on or mirror. Best-selling author Susan Chernak McElroy, in her book *Animals as Teachers and Healers*, discusses how the animals around her developed similar physical maladies to her own. I've witnessed the same. One situation involved a dog who contracted cancer.

Buster was a golden retriever adopted by Lance. They were inseparable. Buster liked to share walks around his complex, trips to the park, and pretzels with his owner late at night. When Buster was diagnosed with cancer, Lance was shocked. Buster died within a year, and soon after, Lance contracted a similar cancer. Lance faced his own mortality, looked at some of the issues prevalent in his life, and survived. He got another retriever to help him through the process. But was Buster's cancer coincidence? Did the dog choose to take on the illness for his owner, providing a catalyst for Lance to look at issues raised by Buster's illness? Perhaps. Some alternative health practices teach that illness begins at the energetic and emotional levels. If not addressed, the disease filters down into the physical body and manifests as ailments.

Unfortunately, Lance did not face his issues until he faced his own cancer and mortality just a short time after losing Buster. But this case is not the only time such a manifestation occurred. More commonly, when people feel unable to cope, their animals take on emotional issues. The problems vary and include conflict between partners, fear of failure, feelings of not being good enough, and lack of control.

The most significant issues arising within a public forum, such as a dog training class, are ones concerning lack of control and feelings of failure. Many people experience frustration when they first learn dog training techniques. Old feelings from childhood arise when students lack coordination, speed, or clarity. Hence, they feel overwhelmed. This feeling is out of proportion to the present situation and acts as a gentle persuader to dive deeper. If the students consciously explore, they release those issues. My colleagues also experience similar situations with their students.

Eventually, I alerted my students to the process before we even started class. Because about one out of ten people struggled with feelings of inadequacy during dog training, it made it easier for those people to forge ahead. When it was explained prior to training, the issue ceased to surface so drastically. Instead, it began to elicit laughter and a big sense of relief for those who combated the unresolved issues that reared their ugly heads during class.

Learning to train animals is like studying to play the piano. Piano lessons require learning how to read notes. Next you learn the keys and how they are played within the arrangement. Ultimately, it takes lots and lots of practice. Who expects to play a concerto within a few weeks? A beginner cannot compare himself to a professional pianist. So why would a person expect to be as adept at dog training as someone who has trained and practiced animal training for all of his or her adult life? People in the workplace struggle with similar issues. They think something should be easy and then torture themselves over what they cannot do rather than praise themselves for what they can do.

This same concern comes up when people want to connect with animals. Otters need persistence to experience success. They may dive over and over again in their search for food. Grooming their fur takes time and effort to get it to the cleanliness level they need to stay warm and healthy. Otters get better with practice and continue their efforts until they succeed. Learning to communicate and understand animals requires the same consistent, unrelenting effort. This endeavor is tough even for veterans.

For instance, I helped a zoo supervisor relocate to another state for a new position at a different facility. While there, I received an invitation to submit an animal behavior consulting estimate. The zoo requested I assess various enclosures and animal behavior issues. First, I observed. Some of the keepers had been working with their charges for years. However, even though the handlers were experienced, they did not see clearly. In one particular situation, the sea lion looked as if he were being taught to vocalize. The trainer gave a command, the sea lion opened his mouth, and then the trainer rewarded him. Next, the trainer moved to a different location and went through the same routine. The animal responded correctly from my point of view, and obviously the sea lion made the same deduction. However, although it appeared the trainer wanted the sea lion to open his mouth to speak, the trainer explained later that he was trying to train the sea lion to stay!

I changed a few techniques and gave the trainer guidance, and he was able to forge ahead and obtain clarity. Consequently, he enjoyed clearer communication with his charge. (You'll find some of the same tips I shared with him in chapter 8.) Learning to communicate, seeing the lessons an animal is sharing, or understanding the grace of spirituality does not happen the first time. It takes practice and requires letting go of expectations. Being consistent and persistent leads you to your ultimate goal.

Healing through Life Experiences

Animals allow people to explore and heal emotional issues when they lack the opportunity through other life experiences. Animals become valued family members, surrogate children, and catalysts for personal development for everyone, but they provide unique growth opportunities for individuals who choose not to marry, not to have children, or not to live in a family situation.

Karen is a loving person and shares her home with a husband and an assortment of creatures. Throughout her married life of more than twenty-five years, at least six animals have lived with her at any given time. She rescues, pet sits, and loves every critter she encounters, but she doesn't feel the same about people.

When asked about her feelings, she commented, "I am more compassionate toward animals. They are vulnerable and honest. They are also dependent on us for everything. I feel immense love for them that I don't for humans." Her household currently supports two dozen animals. This menagerie includes equine, canine, feline, avian, and rodent companions. Karen supports many animal organizations and is constantly surrounded by her animal "children." She makes no apologies in stating, "They are my children of choice."

Karen's animals respond positively to visitors and behave well. They contentedly sleep on, around, or in close proximity to her. They are family and receive kindness and respect. They get all the perks any child might. Every month, Karen's animals go to the groomer, and most attended school for manners. A few received home schooling. The critters get regular veterinary checkups, dental care, and excursions. A jaunt to the nearby forest is the favorite activity. Karen has fought against being a domestic culinary artist by refusing to cook. However, after she learned how an enhanced diet is advantageous to her precious pets, she now manages to cook for them on a daily basis.

Through her "family," she endured the trials of staying up with a sick "child." She worked through petty jealousies among the critters and with her husband. She worried about the dog's progress in "school," lost sleep when her cat became sexually mature, and became socially involved with the humans whose animals are the friends of her own critters. Just as many people find their lives intertwined with those of their children, so too is Karen's life intertwined with the lives of her animals.

Most of us know people like Karen. Her bond with her animals is her link to the world and a connection to her own form of spirituality. She jokingly talks about her meditative "scoop the poop" process, a calming activity that allows her to mull over the current concerns in her life. Karen unites with spirit through her animal activities. These include walks in the woods, caretaking chores, and quiet times with her animals piled on and around her. She finds a deep sense of love, connection, and peace through animals.

Karen is a good example of someone who found her sacred space and spiritual practices in a nontraditional manner. Although religious teachings talk about not judging one another, people often judge Karen. Human prejudice is one of the reasons Karen prefers a household of animals to one of humans.

Honoring One Another

One of the things animals do very well is honor one another. Just as human traditions vary between cultures and spiritual practices, each species sports a different set of rules. Human families develop their own rules over time, and learning to honor and respect others is an important, but often overlooked, element.

In the crowded cities of southern California, many people do not know their neighbors. But in the American South, people invite strangers to come sit on the porch and visit. They sit with you and indulge in a chat and some "sweet tea," a heavily sugared iced tea beverage. In Mexico, household activities stop while inhabitants greet a new guest. Even young children file up to shake the guest's hand before resuming play. These types of practices are examples of honoring the God in everyone. They show reverence to the spark of divinity held deep within. Although taking steps to give tribute to others is important, it is also essential to revere the very best of your own self. In this communication-driven era, many humans ignore or fail to recall proper etiquette. But, as the popular saying states, "elephants never forget!"

Elephants live in large family groups led by the oldest and wisest female. They have great memories, live long lives, and work cooperatively to nurture and assist others within their unit. These herd animals care for one another and get excited when reuniting, even after a short absence. Arrival is heralded through an array of chirping, rumbling, running, trumpeting, and caressing. Trunks intertwine, tails swish, and ears flap. It is a sight to behold.

Wise humans can learn from the elephant example. Take a moment away from projects, the piles on the desk, television, cell phones, and other activities and instead focus on family and friends. Animals are good teachers and examples to follow because they are dependent upon one another for survival. They do not take any relationship for granted. This pattern is repeated in many animal societies.

Wolves, for instance, live within a hierarchy. There is a code to which they adhere. Rules dictate how they greet one another, which wolf eats first, and other related gestures of rank or recognition. A wolf pack engaged in a greeting ritual exhibits certain etiquette; the top-ranking animal is greeted with whining, wagging tails, and licking around the muzzle. When it comes to dinner, the dominant animal eats first. Dogs exhibit the same behaviors, not only among one another, but also with humans. Many dogs jump up on people as they attempt to greet the person. They need to reach the mouth to accomplish the task.

Dogs drop everything to greet anyone coming into their home. They are great examples of how to win friends and influence people! With few exceptions, their greetings are reciprocated with smiles and physical affection. Each evening in homes throughout the world, animals enthusiastically greet their people. The intensity is the same whether the absence has been only a few hours or a few days. Animals respect one another and their owners.

Some humans forget to honor their guests or show simple etiquette to others. Veronica lamented over how her ex-boyfriend seldom showed any signs of enthusiasm when she arrived to visit. "He could be reading a book on the couch and not even look up when I came in. But his dogs! They rushed to meet me at the gate, bodies writhing, tails wagging a million miles a minute. They made me feel like I was the most important person in the world at that moment. It struck me as odd that I felt more valued by them than I did by him."

Animals honor each other and the people they meet. As catalysts for emotional and spiritual development, animals are of great value. Take the story of George, for instance, an engineer who lived alone. The victim of an abusive and emotionally absent mother, he feared starting an intimate relationship, until he met Cleo. Cleo was his cat. He had no say in the matter. She just picked him and planted herself on his doorstep until he relented. Even though she was smaller than a rat, her purr reverberated loudly. How could he resist such a sweet, vulnerable little creature? Soon, Cleo was firmly entrenched in George's life.

They ate together, slept together, and simply hung out together. When asked how she helped him, George said, "I just felt loved for who I was. No matter what kind of day I had, what kind of mood I was in, or how bad things felt, there she was. Gazing at me with those big yellow eyes, purring so loudly that it resonated through my whole body. She'd refuse to leave me alone until I picked her up, petted her, or let her lie on my chest. Even her drooling and sharp kneading became endearing to me. It made me feel lovable, and I felt the love I had for her. I realized I had a lot to give and I began to believe I was worthy of such a deep love."

Love can allow the imaginative and playful part of a person to blossom. New pet owners often become more active. Those with horses or dogs find they lose weight, spend more time out in the fresh air, take risks, and even act more childlike. For instance, they invent excuses for a pet's birthday bash. Their social circle includes other animal owners, and so they spend more time involved in activities with others just as passionate about their pets.

Our animals are motivators and enthusiastic partners. They love us and accept us for all our shortcomings. Part of our journey up the spiritual ladder is to merge with the Divine and get to the point where we experience self-acceptance and self-love. If a person has not chosen a human life partner to assist in this process, then animals can serve as those mirrors that reflect the true self during the climb. The reflection reveals a wonderful person. As we move further up the spiritual ladder, animals echo what we should know, until we get a glimpse of reality, unite the separated parts of ourselves, and reconnect to the celestial blueprint of our higher selves. The main journey is the link back to the Divine.

Otters and other animals are unyielding. The otter uses a rock to break through barriers to get the nourishment he or she needs on a physical level. This determination symbolizes a need to break through both physical and emotional barriers for humans. Passion for life is in an animal's every moment. When animals get excited, they are similar to children. It is hard to say no and disappoint them. If you intend to ask a dog to go for a walk, don't ask unless you are ready, otherwise the pup will relentlessly torment you until you acquiesce. Passion for pets ignites the flame of human caretakers. This helps pet owners overcome any fears or hesitations that prevent participation in extracurricular activities.

Mary's schedule required she get up early, drink a quick cup of coffee, and rush to the office. Her mornings and afternoons were spent on the freeways in bumper-to-bumper traffic. She dreaded each day under the fluorescent lights. Her only highlights were meals, and her weight began to climb. One day while the freeway was gridlocked, she took an alternate route. Movement caught her eye. Below, she glimpsed horses housed adjacent to the road. She thought about her childhood, when, like many young girls, she dreamt about having a horse. Mary's childhood room was crammed with horse books, figurines, and toys, but the dream never materialized. Throughout the day, recollections of childhood flooded her memory. Finally she relented, and instead of sitting in the evening commuter traffic, she drove into the horse ranch.

"My life changed drastically with a simple step. I began taking riding lessons. I was really bad, but I kept at it. I got to know many of the boarders housing their horses at the stable. Soon, I began getting invitations to ride their extra steeds or to join them on the trails. Eventually, one of my favorite horses came up for sale, and the rest is history. My friends changed, my body changed, and I am happier. It was my dream come true."

Mary now rides every weekend. Creative scheduling allowed her to work three or four long days instead of five. "My life is more in balance now. My horse, Sable, and I share an incredible partnership, and I spend as much time with her as I can. I feel alive and playful."

Childhood dreams and living in balance are not the only things animals can catalyze. The creative juices can also create a life filled with animal-related activities. People whose pets inspire them delve into their creativity. They paint, write, and discover new activities and even businesses through their love for their pets. Intense affection opens people up to divine inspiration, and it sparks a youthful sense of adventure and wonder.

Carla lived alone in southern California. Fair-weather friends were all she seemed to find. So, she rescued a small dog. The mutt suffered from numerous health challenges; allergies and dry skin were just some of his struggles. In her quest to help her dog get healthy and stay healthy, she discovered natural diets and alternative practitioners. Throughout the process, she ventured out with Barker to develop his social life. They spent lots of time at dog parks, dog beaches, and in other pet-friendly locations. They indulged in pet and owner activities, and Carla soon met people with the same love and concern for animals.

She said, "Then one day it struck me. Why didn't I just open a dog specialty store? I thought it was a brilliant idea, because it would attract the types of people with the same interests and love for pets."

Unlike pet stores, Barker's Bakery featured specialty nutrition products, holistic foods, snacks, and related items. Carla's idea blossomed into a booming business. Her dog? Well, his health turned around, and Barker loves his job as the official greeter of "his" store.

Pet events and activities are great social outlets for pet people. Mark explained, "I don't like the competitive dog-breed shows, because the competition is stiff and I hate political pressure. Pet shows, goofy events, dog walks, and pet places, such as dog parks, are my favorites. I go for fun, and I've made a lot of new friends as a result. Many share the same interests, and so we might venture out to a specialty store, sign up for a 10K walk, or do something similar. It is an ideal way to make new acquaintances or friends. The people I meet seem more friendly and honest than those I meet elsewhere."

Human social needs motivate people to seek out places where they can find like-minded individuals. Spiritual or religious centers are ideal places to meet others, and many people form strong alliances within those organizations. For those interested in fostering relationships resonating with their own spiritual beliefs or stage of development, these locations provide opportunities to make new acquaintances and to nurture friendships with those who share similar interests and core beliefs. Mark found these same opportunities with other animal lovers.

Pet-related activities, volunteer opportunities with animal organizations, conservation-oriented groups, and animal sports or training activities provide social opportunities for those of like minds and similar interests. Animals actually encourage risk taking. They gently prod their people to form liaisons because it is good for the pet.

The caretaking process means the human owner is responsible for the animal's every need. In good relationships, the motivation is to provide not only physical comfort, but also psychological care and social needs outside of the emotional connection with the owner. In this manner, pets inspire us to embark on a path of selflessness, where we act in the best interest of the other being. Animals need friends and activities to stimulate their minds and contribute to a healthy existence. Often, busy pet owners come up with unique ways to entertain and occupy their pets. People spend whatever time and resources are needed to provide the comfort, care, and stimulation animals require—without a second thought.

Doggie daycare is a popular pursuit. Working pet owners drop off their pooches for a day of romping, snacking, and additional activities with other companion animals. These establishments require formal applications and screen new arrivals for current vaccinations, compatibility with other animals, possible behavioral challenges, and special nutritional needs. The monitored play areas place animals with others of similar age and temperament. Some lucky dogs go every day, while other pooches go once a week. Gwen said, "My dog knows when it is daycare day. She gets very excited and can't wait for us to leave. Once in the car, she can hardly control herself. She doesn't care that I leave her! She is excited about going to see her friends. It is a good feeling to know that I can go run errands while she is busy playing and romping with her pals at the daycare facility."

Our animals spark the creative process and encourage us to "be as little children." Exploring possibilities and seeing the wonder around them is something children do well, but adults shut down. Pets give us permission to reconnect with creativity and childlike qualities. Animals encourage us to take risks, force us to play more, and allow ourselves to explore new creative activities or ventures.

In some cases, it is the search for the unique gift for the little darling that sparks an industry. Victoria decided to use her love of animals to create a unique home business and take advantage of the Internet commerce opportunity. Soon she formed a company with specialty items for pet owners. Products included matching jackets for dog and owner, swank covers for dog beds, imported animal jewelry, and other accessories. When launching her firm, she searched for elegant models. Purebred animals fit the image she wanted perfectly. Afghans, borzois, Chihuahuas, and even some mutts now pose as "fashion hounds." The joke is that they are "real dogs," playing on the phrase some people use to describe someone as ugly. Victoria said, "I always admired one lingerie company's catalog, and I realized how quickly the company grew. The key components to their success were the lovely models and the unique and beautiful products. One day I gazed at my Afghan hounds wearing their custom-made jackets and thought, 'I could do the same thing!' That is how the whole business came into being."

Through our own spiritual growth, we recognize our animals are individuals with unique needs. As a result, our lives with animals become more sophisticated and complex. Twenty-five years ago, few businesses catered to pets. Pet behavior therapy and animal therapy for humans are popular enterprises today. The living conditions of our pets have changed along with the times, as well. Whereas dogs once lived outside and cats dwelled in the barn, these critters now hold integral roles as family members. They get their own beds, playpens, and distinct products for their complex lives. For a time, people believed animals needed to remain at home. Now they journey with their owners to hospitals to cheer the infirm or embark on traveling adventures with their people.

Most fabulous felines and other animals remain homebodies, but this, too, is changing. John said, "I take my cat out with me all the time in her cushy travel carrier, with a leash and a harness. If I am at a timeshare or hotel catering to pets, I sit outside with her tethered to a line so she doesn't get lost and so I can keep an eye on her. She'll eat grass, sniff around, or just come and lounge with me, and I enjoy it. I travel constantly. It does not seem fair to leave her alone, so I bring her along. We take walks, mostly in quiet places, because wayward dogs create a hazard."

Going with the Flow

Our interactions and views on domestic animals have changed, and those concerning wild animals and the environment have, too. We are all strands in the web of life. If you impact one, the others tremble along with it. The longing for a deeper connection with nature, and understanding our place within it, has manifested as an industry of wild animal pets.

The motivations for owning a wild animal vary. Some people want the animals for the status, the illusion of power associated with ownership, or the unrealistic expectations of what the association will be like. Wild or exotic animals require complex environments, intricate social connections, specialized diets and veterinary care, and unique housing. In many areas, special permits are compulsory. The commitment and complexity of managing these critters is beyond the average person's ability, and many of the animals end up in dire straits. If the animal is among the lucky few, it is relinquished to an agency dedicated to such tragedies.

Even so, some wild specimens have infiltrated the pet industry. In the past, untamed animals were imported and smuggled in for sale as pets. This detrimental practice harmed animals and their environments, and in some cases still does. However, there are specialty breeders who provide wild critters to the pet trade. More and more exotic creatures, especially birds and reptiles, are finding their way into households around the United States.

Although ownership of avian pets and reptilian companions is not as widespread as dogs and cats, they occasionally appear in public with their owners. Fred said, "As an exotic pet owner, I am cautious about exposing my animal to others. But I don't feel the relationship is much different from a close bond with a dog or a cat. We enjoy each other's company and want to socialize. I think the animals find it interesting and stimulating."

Relationships with wild animals cannot be compared to those of our domestic companions; they are altogether different. Wild critters are finely tuned to survival of the fittest. As such, they maintain their wildness even when in a captive environment. They remain independent and take advantage of any opportunities—unlike domestic animals, who are bred for their cooperative behavior and will acquiesce to us.

People who want to control or conquer a wild animal often desire a sense of omnipotence. They crave an elusive connection which they can't define, but is not satisfied by the average pet. The more they attempt to grasp, the further they are from success. When working with wild animals you cannot always control what transpires. You must disengage from any attachments and let go of expectations. "Go with the flow" and "Let go and let God" mean not trying to force your will, but moving toward a higher force, an exalted will. Disharmony is exhibited through control issues and is often mirrored by the animals in the lives of those struggling to move through the lesson. If animals don't mirror it, they definitely create an opportunity for us to look at our own issues.

Martin trained dolphins under contract for the United States Navy. In the program, the dolphins accompanied the trainer's boat out into the open ocean, where they engaged in various studies that examined their capacities and sensitivities to the environment, such as sound pollution from boats, oil rigs, and related equipment. Martin and I regularly discussed the challenges of animal training in both the captive environment and the open ocean, and we compared notes while challenging each other to be more innovative and insightful with our charges. Through these discussions we brainstormed solutions to behavioral problems. Although some of Martin's projects were confidential, without revealing any secrets, he asked me my opinion about his sessions, inviting me to share how I might have handled difficult situations he encountered.

One such discussion involved a female dolphin with whom he shared a great working relationship. He treated all his trainees with fairness, but he struggled with his attachment to how this dolphin should perform. He did not allow for any variations or idiosyncrasies. Adhering to standards in animal training is important, but animals experience good days and bad days, too. As Martin described his interactions with the dolphin during his sessions in the open ocean, he began to pontificate.

Although Martin is incredibly intuitive at times, he conveyed an unbending attitude and strict adherence to training theory in this situation. When the dolphin refused to fully cooperate, Martin became single-minded and began coercing her instead of working with her. Expressing his shock over her reaction, he rhetorically asked me, "What do you think she did then?" I laughed and said, "If I were the dolphin, I would have ditched you and headed out to open ocean." And of course, that is what she had done. She essentially gave him a time-out.

This provided Martin with the opportunity to let go of his attachments. He fumed for a while, but he also was concerned about her safety. A lone dolphin faces many dangers in the sea. When Martin's boat finally arrived back at his base, the dolphin was waiting for him at the entrance to the cetacean holding areas.

Animals help us in areas where we need personal growth. Martin's particular learning curve involved issues about flexibility and open-mindedness. He needed to realize the world is colorful and that there also are shades of gray—not just black and white. The dolphin got fed up with him and decided to help accelerate his lesson about cooperative behavior, acceptance, and letting go—by leaving him floating in the middle of the ocean. This gave him time to contemplate and shift his attitude. There is no real control over other beings; it is an illusion.

While the dolphin exemplified the lesson of letting go, otters adeptly illustrate the message "Go with the flow" as they float and play in the current. Honoring others and the lessons they need to experience helps accelerate the growth process and builds momentum to move to the next rung of the spiritual climb.

3

Power of the Polar Bear

The white bear towered over the tundra as he rose up on his hind legs to sniff the air. In this white world, his large statuesque figure was virtually invisible to the eye. As he moved his head back and forth to sample the breeze, only his dark nose and beady eyes gave away his presence. As his powerful snout caught the scent of a seal, it quivered slightly. Lowering his massive torso, he loped toward what might be a rich meal.

Of all the animals I've encountered, the polar bear is a formidable predator, afraid of nothing, not even humans. I've heard stories from pilots who guarded their equipment and passengers against these animals, and from people who watched these bears work against barriers to try to get at a researcher or photographer encased and protected by a measly little cage. Polar bears accept life in a harsh environment by

> Polar bears accept life in a harsh environment by adapting to it. With strength and stamina, they own their power. These animals embody a strong sense of self and rely on their instincts. Like polar bears, we can move into personal power, self-acceptance, and confidence. Accepting our strength taps us into the power of the Divine.

adapting to it. With strength and stamina, they own their power. These animals embody a strong sense of self and rely on their instincts. They live life without having to consort with others of their kind, except for brief interludes.

The polar bear exemplifies the qualities we find on the third rung of the spiritual ladder. On this step, we learn to honor our intuition and ourselves, to throw away our need for external approval, and to accept our life for what it is, with all its challenges. Our lessons emerge as we learn from our trials. We then move into personal power, self-acceptance, and confidence. Accepting our strength taps us into the power of the Divine and into the universal flow.

Today there is a lot of emphasis and validation around being a victim, someone without personal power. The world can be harsh, and it usually is not fair, but the challenges we face make us stronger if we move beyond them. The secret to success is to adapt to the changing environment in the same way animals do. If there is a storm in your life, you may need to burrow, move to higher ground, or brace yourself against it. How you deal with it is a choice. But if you take no action, accept no responsibility, then you make a choice, a statement to the universe. Healing takes time and the process requires movement, but if you wallow in sorrow, anger, or fear, you close yourself off to the divine flow.

When I first heard the saying, "Life is not for sissies," it made me laugh. However, it is true. As we move through life, we should grow and advance through our experiences. If not, these lessons get repeated. I remember facing harassment in the workplace. I did what I thought best and was penalized. Later, in another work environment, I experienced another similar challenge. I wondered why I faced it again. I figured I didn't get the lesson. Sometimes we are so close to a situation that we fail to recognize we are on an endless loop. Animals get stuck in loops too, and they show us just how crazy it can get.

Aberrant behavior in captive animals is usually a sign of too much stress or that something else is wrong. Poor exhibit design, disharmonious animal groupings, lack of mental stimulation, or physical illness can contribute to deviant behavior. Stereotypic behavioral exhibitions involve detrimental and abnormal repetitive patterns. You probably have observed bears or large cats endlessly pacing back and forth, or in circles, often tossing their heads when they turn. Perhaps you witnessed an otter or a sea lion swimming in repetitive patterns, or a dog mutilating its body. These animals are caught in the loop. The only way out is to get to the root of the problem and deal with it. The same is true for our life lessons.

Another lesson involves being secure enough to be authentic, no matter what the circumstances. When people overwhelmingly need the approval of others, they are not true to themselves and lack personal power. Incarcerated in a jail of their own devising, they are surrounded by bars of low self-worth or lack of respect for themselves or others. In some cases, these people find inappropriate groups, such as gangs or cults, to identify with. Instead of developing a healthy self-image, they glom onto the accepted activities of others and never develop a strong identity as an individual. Animals own a sense of self, no matter what the circumstances or the environment.

One of my first encounters with a captive polar bear occurred at a large zoo in southern California. Animals in zoos are sometimes managed not by the type of animal but by different areas. Each section contains a variety of species of animals housed within, and every institution sorts their collection differently. At the time, I rotated through all the different areas so I learned the zoo-keeping routines and what animals resided within each zone. When I got to the keeper area behind the polar bear exhibit, it reminded me of a prison.

The back entry door was constructed of heavy steel and mesh. The doors leading to the exhibit from the polar bear night quarters were also heavy metal and controlled by substantial levers and cables in the keeper pathway. Everything else was cement.

As we began to move the doors to allow the animal access to the outside, the hair on my neck stood straight up. Without viewing the bear, I sensed danger. Then I noticed that, unlike some of the other exhibits and divisions I worked in, no viewing windows existed to watch the bear's movement. When I asked the head keeper about it, he explained the bear was an intense killer and attempted to ambush any keeper working the area. Keepers could only view the animal by removing the heavy steel plates covering the mesh-enforced windows. The bear destroyed previous windows and now they took extra safety precautions.

The keeper slid the window open, and although we hoped the bear had moved into the exhibit, we found ourselves nose to snout with the massive creature. Apparently he wanted a whiff of me. My gut informed me of his ill intent and the keeper confirmed this bear was a surly character. The bear took pleasure in hiding in those areas not easily viewed through the windows and worked at ambushing the careless, and as a result, only a few people worked the exhibit. The polar bear wasn't malicious; he was true to his nature. A polar bear is simply one of the most powerful predators around, and because polar bears don't have anything that preys on them, they are intensely curious—not fearful. The bear's prison was a physical one, but he had a strong sense of who he was, possessing not only physical strength but also psychological strength and spirit. He was, at his core, a truly wild carnivore.

Adapting to the Environment

Another wild carnivore with unique talents is the cat. Its allure has captured us and prompted close relationships between humans and domesticated felines. All animals help us in similar ways, but the cat exudes the confidence and self-esteem found on this rung of growth.

Cats are completely at ease with themselves, direct about what they want, and secure that they will get it. Watch a cat for a day to get a glimpse into what it is like to be in trust and power.

Cats are comfortable with themselves. Felines do not lack self-worth and do what they want, how they want, and when they want. They oblige their humans, but some cats definitely feel they own the world. Like other animals, they are loving and accepting of any human faults or mistakes. Our feline companions have a zest for life and a knack for priorities (theirs). But if we pay attention, they can teach us lessons about honoring what we need and want.

Boots, a black-and-white tomcat, displays an intrinsic need to hunt outside. Even though his owner, Ruth, prefers Boots to be an indoor cat, she realizes it is an impossible task. After ten years, she has given up. "My husband, friends, and I all fail miserably at keeping him in. Poised on a chair in the kitchen, he rushes out when we are in the midst of chores. He prepares to dash through the front door when he hears the key in the lock and my arms are full of groceries. He demands visitors let him out, and they do! And when all else fails, he finds an open window and busts through the screen."

Boots is more accommodating when it comes to something he wants, such as food or attention. However, he still is the naughty kitty who won't think twice about getting under the sink into the trash to steal any leftover tidbits from dinner, an empty tuna can, or even the package remains from the butcher. "He asks for what he wants, but if we tell him to wait, then he does. He sits in the sun, lounges nearby, and sometimes asks again nicely. This is opposite to his frenzy to escape to the outdoors."

Animals educate us about the acceptance of self, of others, and of situations beyond our control. The polar bear accepts his harsh life in the wild without any qualms. Although cats seem more selective about whom they let into their inner sanctum, they do eventually accept others. New household additions, whether animals or humans, must go through a grace period.

Marcy, an avid animal lover and pet groomer, said, "My animals are always good judges of character. If they don't warm up to someone after a period of time, I take a closer look at the person. Using animal-like discernment makes my life much easier. I wait and watch before labeling someone new in my life as a friend. More often than not, that action prevents heartaches and business and personal complications. Now my new human pals are in alignment with who I am. We build stronger foundations over time and truly share similar values and interests."

Some animals roll with change and acclimatize. Take the clever coyote. While many animal populations suffer from human destruction of the environment, encroachment on their territories, or persecution, the coyote has adapted and thrived. Coyote populations moved into areas not previously occupied, and the small canines do quite well near human settlements. These animals live mainly in pairs, or small family groups, and in my youth I very seldom saw large aggregations of this critter. Now I see hefty groups of coyotes gathering together on a regular basis. They adapt and flourish through scavenging and hunting. Much to the dismay of many suburbanites, coyotes developed a strategy to lure unattended family pets out into areas where other pack members can dispatch them quickly.

Coyotes teach us to accept life for what it is and move with it. If we cannot change circumstances, it is up to us to find ways to adapt. Some animals take longer to do so, but in order to survive they must. Survival of the fittest means only those who can and do change will live to see the future. Our situation is not always a matter of survival—we have choices. We can choose our environment, our friends, and our actions. When we see the possibilities and make the best of them, rather than focusing on the adversities, we enter into the right current.

Animals show us such lessons from different perspectives, too. Sure, some animals don't do too well with change. Many of those difficulties usually stem from changes in a predictable routine or a big life shift. Moving, for instance, is a trauma for many animals, while others accept changes contentedly. The difference between the two responses often is rooted in how complex or stimulating the environment is, and the degree of bonding the animal has with the human.

When Nancy and Frank moved their menagerie from the mountains to the beach, most of their animals adjusted easily. The dogs happily romped on the beach instead of in the woods. They loved the ocean and chasing birds for long stretches of beach. The cats loved the humid air and bright sunlight, which contrasted to the tree-shaded home of their former mountain abode. Only one cat suffered from deep-rooted and severe issues. These stemmed from mental instability and emotional sensitivity, and she didn't adjust well. The rest of the clan remained content and happy.

On the opposite end of the spectrum from the happy menagerie, some animals do not adjust well to moves. For instance, a zoo in California decided to build a new bear exhibit. Money was raised so one of the resident bears could move and enjoy a larger and more versatile environment. The state-of-the-art facility contained every bell and whistle possible, with spectacular viewing stations for the humans and complex enrichment opportunities for the animals. The bears scheduled to occupy the enclosure included one accustomed to life in an old grotto at the zoo, plus orphaned cubs brought to the zoo from the wild. Up until that time, the zoo bear's life was very predictable. He transferred into the exhibit, without enough integration time to allow him, or the other bears, to adapt. Hence, the move caused extreme stress and triggered stereotypic pacing behavior and illness. Although the facility looked good to the human eye, design mistakes and the rush to open it to the public didn't allow for an adequate integration period. As concerns escalated, the use of psychotropic drugs was discussed. Eventually the exhibit errors and the other mistakes were addressed. In the end, no drugs were used on the animals. The initial move included a lot of drama and stress and, unfortunately, the old bear died from it, but the rest survived and adapted.

Although repetitive behaviors also occur in pets due to excessive stress, some animals exhibit similar stereotypic behaviors when they become accustomed to their owners behaving predictably. The animals begin to expect certain activities, and if those activities do not take place, it causes stress. This happens in the case of anticipation. For instance, a dog who expects to eat at a certain time may develop pacing behavior, or barking and whining exhibitions, just prior to feeding. Feeding then reinforces the behavior and it continues to escalate, getting worse over time.

Dogs kept outdoors usually lead boring lives and often lack the strong bonds with their caretakers that dogs living indoors share. Ostracized pets display many more behavior problems than those incorporated into the home. Canines kept outside commonly exhibit problems such as destructive digging, incessant barking, running the fence, or detrimental chewing. Behavior problems communicate that change is needed.

Adopting Right Action

As we grow, it is important to move beyond our need for external approval and live life secure in our own selves. This can be difficult. One of the big societal pressures for many women in the United States concerns the focus on external appearances rather than internal character. Some people are sensitive to what others think and feel about them. Bulimia, anorexia, and other disorders stem, in part, from low self-esteem. Attempting to conform to standards, or to control something through food, is aberrant behavior similar to that exhibited by animals. Some animals regurgitate their food for attention or out of boredom. They usually then consume it again, much to the disgust of people observing.

The holidays are difficult times for many people, especially those who feel ostracized or isolated. Like pets isolated from their owners, these people need a connection. Bonds with family or friends are important, but do we pay attention to people in our communities and congregations? The most fabulous spiritual practices I have experienced involved community events and "orphan parties." People reached out to one another to make sure others knew they were valued.

The first orphan party I attended was held by people I met in college. Their spiritual practice included weekly fireside chats where people of all backgrounds dialogued about different spiritual topics. Because I was not spending the December break with my family, they invited me to attend their holiday party. When I arrived, everyone in attendance was somehow "orphaned" from their families or other significant relationships. The two women who arranged the event truly paid attention to the other people they encountered in life. It was one of the loveliest gatherings of people I have experienced. Like animals, the women relied on their instincts and brought together people who otherwise would have been stressed or alone during the holiday season.

Animals instinctively know the right actions to take. Therapy animals often sit quietly and allow the patients they visit to fuss over them. At other times, they may instigate interactions or reach out to touch the patient. When humans are at a loss for what to say or do, animals just forge right ahead. They trust and rely on their instincts not only for survival but also for right action, something we need to pay closer attention to.

Trusting in ourselves is a significant lesson on this rung of the ladder, too. When I follow my gut feelings, or instincts, I am usually right. Wild animals follow their instincts and intuitions all the time. This is what ensures their survival. As we get to a point where we actually trust in ourselves, things get better. But humans resist change, and resistance creates stress and prevents growth or the opportunity for progress.

In the animal training world, the joke is that the only thing two trainers agree on is that the third trainer is wrong. Traditional animal training practices have endured over long durations of time and some people refuse to explore different techniques. Tried-and-true is better than risking your health and safety, they say, or that of your charges. Training is an art and a science, but the newest trends of positive rein-forcement techniques are actually not new at all. Contemporary efforts are more refined, but back in the 1800s, for example, a zoo man from the Hagenbeck family discovered he achieved better behavior through rewards. He was known for his exceptional and innovative techniques in animal care and training. Even so, domestic dogs are still trained with techniques that became popular just after World War II. I prefer the more contemporary, and less forceful, adaptations.

Humans resist change all the time. When I first learned to work on a computer, the smallest one took up a whole room. I love most of the changes computers bring to our daily lives, but some people still refuse to use them. We are meant to adapt and feel secure with our choices. It is not a matter of right or wrong, it is a matter of acceptance. When we come from a center of strength and security, accepting change, or accepting and respecting the choices of others, can be accomplished without feeling that our beliefs and values are under attack.

Moving through Fear into Appreciation

All life has a role in this world. No matter how enthralling or revolting we might perceive an animal to be, every creature contributes some-thing. As we begin to observe, study, or work more closely with animals, our views of life change. The same thing happens when we work with people of other cultures, races, or environments.

Different animals trigger a multitude of reactions from humans. Although hordes of people approach pets, many fear wild animals and even insects. These animals are viewed erroneously, suspiciously, fearfully, and sometimes with resentment.

Ronald, a forest service employee, said, "It always amazes me how removed from reality some people are. There seems to be two different groups—the first come up to the forest and think that bears are like Smokey the Bear, or Yogi Bear, the cartoon characters. They want to pet or feed them and don't view the bear as a wild animal. Then there are the wilderness fans who truly understand what bears can do; they do everything in their power to avoid encounters."

During a drought in southern California, lots of animals entered populated areas to scavenge and search for water. "This brings a higher risk of incidents," Ronald said. "We posted warnings everywhere, because most of our visitors are from the city and are clueless about what a real bear is, or can do. A few years back, a bear entered a campground and pulled a kid out of a tent. That brought people back to a sense of reality."

Mention the words *mountain lion* and city dwellers close to incident areas shudder. The fear of being attacked or eaten is a big one, even though it is only a slight risk. Those who live in wilderness areas often take it in stride that wildlife is nearby. In the Mendocino and Humboldt counties of California, Native Americans and locals took it for granted when curious lions followed them. As we encroach on their habitats and fail to adapt and work at understanding nature, problems do arise. However, facing our fears, sometimes literally, does wonders to dissipate them.

One of the stories Ranger Ronald shared surprised even me. "We get visitors in with strange ideas about how the world should work," he said. "Many people ask us why we don't use insecticide in the forest to get rid of the insects. They really have no idea about the role of these creatures in the balance of nature."

All creatures provide a thread in what is called the "web of life." We are all connected in this way. The relationship requires steward-ship, care, and respect for every living being. Each individual has some-thing important to contribute to the world. Every animal, whether insect, fish, bird, reptile, or mammal, shares lessons and exemplifies how we can live in harmony. In the story of Noah's Ark, animals of every kind were loaded onto the ark to keep them alive through the Flood. They were important then, and they are important now.

Like all other beings, insects, spiders, and ticks play vital roles in keeping nature balanced. Because most people inhabit concrete and asphalt jungles and are removed from living in the nature world, many of them consider predators, rodents, and insects to be nuisance animals. Mention insects or anything that creeps or crawls and reactions range from fascination to annoyance, fear, or even hatred.

When I taught a comparative animal science course for a private institution, students learned about the rainforest and the life within it while observing contrasts in the local mountains and surrounding regions of southern California. The uniqueness of the insects and their relatives fascinated the students. Although insects annoy or inconven-ience many humans, they also play vital roles to assist us.

Insects contribute to the food on our plates and in our pantries through their roles in pollinating crops. Our relationship with honey-bees began over 12,000 years ago in ancient Mesopotamia. Honey for our table and wax for cosmetics, creams, and candles are just a few of their contributions.

Long before we thought about recycling, nature provided us with examples. Beetles, ants, flies, maggots, and related insects serve as cleanup crews and recyclers. For eons they have assisted with decom-position of carcasses, debris, and other vegetation, while many also aer-ate the soil. Don't like worms? How about silk? Silkworms have woven their way into the hearts of silk lovers for more than 4,000 years.

Arachnophobia is a fear of spiders. The movie of the same name made lots of people squirm, but spiders, along with some of their insect cousins, serve as specialized predators that assist with biological pest control. Even ticks and beetles help control populations of animals and plants by spreading disease. Without them to act as checks and balances, who knows what troubles we would encounter?

Every nation views animals differently. Although the United States frowns on the consumption of dogs and cats, some people from other cultures consider them a delicacy. It is the same with cows. In America, we consume and use many products from the cattle and dairy industry, but in other countries the cow is sacred. You might hate the thought of flies and ants invading your home, but native peoples used maggots to help heal infections and decapitated ant heads to suture wounds.

Early in my career I served as a naturalist on whale watch trips and provided narratives on marine life and tide pools. At that time, aquariums and oceanariums were novel and first exposed people to marine life. Close encounters with performing whales and dolphins rendered people awestruck. Enthralled with these animals, people formed the impression that cetaceans were mystical and magical; the same fascination has endured for centuries in many cultures.

The story of Jonah tells of how a great fish swallowed him. Jonah remained in its belly until he was vomited up on the shore three days later. Greek tales tell of Delphinos, a dolphin sea-god, who fetched a bride for Poseidon. In reward for his service, Delphinos was placed among the stars as the constellation Delphin. Both Shakespeare's *Twelfth Night* and fifth-century historian Herodotus recount the story of Arion, a boy who played music for the dolphins. They dived, leaped, and danced in the waves in response to his tunes. The dolphins even followed him on a journey that turned sour. To escape, Arion leapt from the ship onto the back of a dolphin and rode home safely.

In addition to tales of the benevolence of dolphins, accounts exist about people who were pushed out to sea or attacked by these animals sporting a perpetual smile. Even though dolphins are not the trained Flipper of the television series, people want to believe they are. Nature is a serious teacher and captures us with her complexities, mysteries, and power. As we stand on the earth, we are connected. The more we become removed from our daily interactions with animals and the life around us, the more we crave it. Animals lure us to come closer. People are curious and want to meet the critters with so many unique and fascinating adaptations to life.

Moving through our fear and into trusting ourselves and divine guidance is perhaps the final stage before we reach acceptance and detachment, where we can observe and no longer judge. The steps to move through fear involve becoming calm and centered. We must observe from a distance through the eyes of our higher selves.

We can learn some of these techniques by watching a cat keeping its balance, taking things in stride, observing its surroundings, and maintaining intense but graceful movements while intent on hunting; these activities can remind us to stay unruffled and focused. Becoming trustful requires that we move through more layers.

Learning to trust demands vulnerability, but vulnerability built on a foundation of understanding of self and of those who are different from us. This learning requires a mental shift to abandon our assumptions and speculations. Knowledge that comes with growth recognizes the shades of difference between discernment and discrimination.

In the natural world there is a focus on survival, so animals do discriminate. Many bristle against strangers and some destroy the weak. Predators cull populations by selecting the sick, young, disabled, or old. Animal mothers feed the strong, and when food is in short supply, they may abandon their brood altogether. Humans can assess their choices and select alternatives to fear or aversion.

Interactions with animals such as spiders and snakes are stepping-stones toward bigger issues. Each person has his or her own hurdles to address. Sometimes the hurdle is forgiveness, letting go, or becoming more accepting. Bigger issues may include themes related to racial, gender, sexual, or age discrimination. However, usually our lessons surface in areas where we feel "lesser than." Much of it starts with your own self. Can you look in the mirror and see the divinity reflected back? Can you truly say you love yourself? Or do you only see what is wrong with the reflection?

The polar bear lives in a world of pure reflection and light. He accepts himself and his surroundings. He claims it all, and so everything is transparent: the water, the ice, and even the hollow shafts of his fur. The sunlight around him can blind those not adjusted to it. But his stamina takes him through all the seasons. When fatigue or annoyance troubles many people during the long days when the sun shines around the clock, the polar bear remains impassive. The bear relies on all his senses, and everything is illuminating for the animal who owns his power. He represents an example of clarity, insight, the larger perspective, an uncluttered view, and the ability to distance oneself from the world. He exhibits a variety of survival and hunting strategies, learns quickly, and is immensely patient.

When you own your power, then the past does not control your actions. You see things with clarity and so you can get a different, and larger, perspective. If you visit your old schoolroom as an adult, you might marvel at how small it is, even though your memory screams that it was bigger. Revisiting memories can lessen their hold on you. Changing your views can take you forward to a place where you can review painful or disturbing memories without wincing or cringing. Like the bear, you can lumber up the icy glacier to get above the frozen emotions for an uncluttered view. Scrutinizing from the top shows you how painful experiences took you higher as you overcame them. Your efforts to get to the pinnacle lift you up and move you closer to the Divine.

It is from this vantage point that you can grasp the insights that come and distance yourself from things that obscure your gut reactions or true impressions. From the summit you can take old survival strategies and hone them into skills, move forward, replace archaic tactics with effective ones, and find patience with yourself and others. New tactics enable you to be an esteemed hunter not only of personal power but also of power from a higher source. Invigoration helps you trek to the next level of spiritual growth.

Getting through these lessons requires self-acceptance first. Then, as we move forward, perhaps from our new vantage point we can glimpse acceptance of everyone and move into a space of love and understanding. From there, we can approach the next level on the ladder of spiritual growth, where we learn from the lion.

4

Heart of the Lion

Highlighted with rich, deep-chocolate-colored spots, the mountain lion's pelt would fade into a lovely tan color and retain only a few dark highlights by the time he reached six months of age. Even though he was only a couple of months old, he resisted having his photo taken with all his might. In the end, I held him up by the scruff of his neck as he cocked his ears back in annoyance. Only slightly bigger than a house cat, the mountain lion was all muscle and was already equipped with teeth and claws capable of serious damage. His eyes glowered as he hissed and spat. His size did not matter; he had the heart of lion—filled with innate courage.

> Lions above all are courageous. They avoid fights but are not afraid to face their opponents or their fears. They are curious creatures, affectionate with one another and passionate with their partners. These creatures conserve their energy for matters of importance and do not worry needlessly. Living from the core is not for the faint of heart.

When most people think of lions, they think of African lions, big beasts who live in family groups called prides. Male African lions sport thick manes that surround and protect their heads and necks. The African lioness is hefty, and these sleek creatures hunt for the whole group and work cooperatively to raise their families. Mountain lions, on the other hand, are smaller, lean felines with stunning black highlights around the nose, cheeks, and ears. The mascara-like markings around and above the eyes give the adult cat a striking appearance. Although these cats are smaller than their more popular African cousin, they make up for their size in heart.

Lions above all are courageous. They avoid fights, but they are not afraid to face their opponents or their fears. Sometimes they even tackle prey animals who outweigh them. They are curious creatures, affectionate with one another and passionate with their partners. Mother lions of both of these species guide, teach, and protect their young. These creatures conserve their energy for matters of importance and do not worry needlessly. They exemplify the lessons to be learned on the fourth rung of the spiritual ladder and provide examples of heartfelt living.

Living from the core is not for the faint of heart, and that is why the lion is such a good example. When we are balanced on this rung, we operate from a center of compassion and love. When we are not harmonious, the arising symptoms include loneliness, jealousy, bitterness, anger, an inability to forgive others, a lack of commitment, and a failure to follow our hearts or protect ourselves emotionally. At this level, we need to come to grips with who we are at present and to love ourselves and those around us.

At a well-known church in San Diego, we recited a simple prayer to remind us of our place on the fourth rung: "Divine love, flowing through me, blesses and multiplies all that I am, all that I have, and all that I receive." The only thing missing from the statement is that divine love also blesses all that we encounter. Love is what catalyzes us into true, deep healing. The emotional pain experienced in our lives can be healed in an instant through love. Sounds great, doesn't it? But it isn't easy getting there. In fact, conscious individuals work at it every day. The steps to experiencing unconditional love involve an ability to forgive, to be compassionate, and to heal old emotional wounds.

Emotionally, one of the hardest jobs is being a worker for an animal services department or shelter. As an adoption counselor for an animal shelter, a person takes in animals and keeps them until they receive homes or become too disturbed to keep any longer. For a short, heart-wrenching time, I was affiliated with a shelter. In some cases, I observed the mental state of animals deteriorate. I was also appalled at the daily number of people wanting to drop off animals, and I found it hard not to judge the actions of others in those situations. My compassionate nature was pained by what I witnessed.

Some of the reasons people dropped off animals included moving to a new home; bringing home a new baby; deciding the animal was too big or too small; finding the animal too active; thinking the animal was too hairy or dirty; or not getting permission from a landlord before acquiring a pet. Few pet owners were willing to do the work necessary to rectify their situations—it was easier to dump the animal. But it was the reaction of the animals that I watched with interest. Animals possess an innate ability to live in the moment and are good examples if you want to learn about trust, hope, love, and the ability to heal.

Although each abandoned or relinquished animal grieved in its own way, most accepted the situation and made the best of it. The animals played, solicited attention, and amused visitors and staff alike with their antics. Many found better homes than they came from, but some suffered mentally and failed to thrive. Despite professional training, this kind of work situation is depressing. I attempted to mask it by exhibiting other emotions and attempting to present a more professional and removed demeanor, but I too am an animal and lousy at masking my emotions. People deal with situations such as these differently. Some engage in behaviors that don't appear logical. One such incident involved a dog named TJ.

I discovered TJ, a pregnant bitch, in the overflow holding area when I came back to work after a day off. Wanda, the kennel manager, told me she just couldn't turn her away. TJ was a scrawny and mangy-looking mutt from the streets. With the body of a corgi, the ears of a coyote, and the wiry fur of a terrier, she was a stout little mongrel who attempted to attack anyone who came near her cage. The only person graced with TJ's acceptance was Wanda. Only Wanda could feed and clean TJ without the threat of attack. From a professional standpoint, I did not understand why Wanda brought this mongrel into the already overstocked shelter, especially since TJ was about to whelp, which meant we could not place her for at least a couple of months. Additionally, the litter of puppies would need placement. My concern was that the puppies would get homes in preference over the older and larger dogs who had resided at the shelter for what seemed like ages.

When TJ finally gave birth to her litter, things got complicated. Now she was not only defensively aggressive but also territorial and offensively aggressive. And if that wasn't enough, she was a lousy mother. The climax came when a few pups slid out of the warm whelping box and onto the cold, hard concrete, their survival threatened by hypothermia. Wanda was not working and so I was elected to perform the rescue. Armed with my physical shield, the metal trashcan lid from the food storage bin, I entered TJ's cage. TJ lunged at me in numerous attempts to attack me while I thwarted her like a gladiator fighting a dwarf. I fumbled around with my other hand, moving the wayward pups back into the warm box. I escaped intact. After the incident, TJ welcomed me into her fold along with Wanda.

Later I realized that Wanda unconsciously took on a project that was good for morale. Everyone fussed over TJ and the pups. In an environment where many animals do not survive physically or mentally, these pups were full of life and brought tears of joy and lots of laughter to the staff, and of course they all found homes. During the process we all moved forward: TJ evolved into a more caring mother and suckered Wanda into taking her home. For me, it made me remember it's the little things that trigger growth and awareness. I believe we overlook the incremental steps to enlightenment or to connecting with our higher selves.

Personally, I reconnected with my emotions despite the overwhelmingly painful and frustrating work environment. Although I recognized I could not remain there, my experiences led me to develop a new program to help abandoned and kenneled animals. I donated the program to a national humane organization and a countrywide animal training network for implementation. The most rewarding parts of my role at the shelter involved connecting with and supporting the animals through their grief. I watched them move forward as they adapted to shelter life, learned better behavior, and (at least for some) finally landed in suitable homes.

Animals fated to a life within a shelter or rescue agency trigger our compassionate natures. Interacting with other animals does, too, but there is something about the helplessness and stark environments of shelter life that moves people to action. Animals require that we give of ourselves—and not just food, water, and housing. When people give of themselves, it makes a huge difference. If we start with animals, then maybe we can move into the home, neighborhood, and community. How many families give of their material goods or finances instead of their time and their emotions? When was the last time you shared a cup of coffee with your neighbor? Do you know the animals in your neighborhood but not the people? The local animals usually know everyone.

Out of Every Adversity Comes Something Good of Equal or Greater Value

Our rescue operation, during Hurricane Georges in Florida, was winding down for the night when an old beat-up Honda drove in. The woman looked frazzled as she got out and headed my way. Her short brown hair stood up in multiple directions, while the humidity caused her clothes to cling tightly to her body, and no shoes protected her feet. She was here for help.

Hurricane flooding had trapped her precious animals in the top floor of her home. We quickly loaded up a few travel crates, and I followed her out to what used to be her neighborhood. The dogs swam out with her husband and he held them on ropes looped around their necks. They were junkyard mongrels loved by her, but dangerous to strangers. As I let her load them into the rescue vehicle, I noticed that, lacking carriers, her friends stuffed the cats into her car. As I drove off, the picture in my rearview mirror reflected the silhouettes of those who had lost their homes. They stood silently with heavy shoulders, toes at the edge of the waters, staring blankly across the aquatic barrier to their past.

Rescue work reveals the very best and the very worst in people. What touched my heart was the faith of the woman. After we safely secured her animals in the veterinary clinic we spoke at length. Her family and friends shared hotel rooms and focused on the good instead of what was lost. Disaster survivors always amaze me. She was an example of what happens when you surrender to divine will instead of fighting it.

During this particular disaster, the Florida community opened their hearts to help one another. Our team shared our expertise, and we spent our time patrolling the muggy environment and helping both domestic pets and the affected wildlife. Almost everyone was warm and supportive, but one of my coworkers showed a closed heart.

Fred was standing with me when the woman in the old Honda drove into our command center. When Fred sneered and muttered about the "trailer trash" woman, I was stunned. Perhaps he was experiencing emotional overload and trying to mask it, as I had done at the shelter, but whatever the root of his comments and reaction, his judgment and hardness made me angry. I was glad he did not interact with the woman and pleased I saw beyond the external appearances. I was not seeing through my eyes, but through my heart.

Being compassionate is something I work at, especially when I get exasperated at the disappearance of common courtesy and the refusal of some individuals to take personal responsibility for their actions and lives. Today many people dwell on their past traumas and dramas instead of working through the issues. Carolyn Myss, the medical intuitive and best-selling author, defines healing as getting over the pain instead of marketing it. We tend to dwell on our old "stuff," and those wounds become a bonding mechanism between people. But animals show us the way to move through the pain to the other side.

Common Struggles, Common Bonds

One of the enjoyable things about teaching a group animal training course is the sense of family that develops. Everyone struggles with the same challenges. How do you hold the leash, concentrate, give the hand signal, and get the behavior all at the same time? As classes progress, students greet each other, help each other, celebrate their successes, and even engage in social events together. Animal training is also therapy for healing old issues, whether people know it or not.

When I began conducting domestic animal training classes, I noticed how some students took the training courses very seriously. Their emotional reactions often took me by surprise. I'd witness students competing with and assisting one another, arguing intensely over what another family member did with the dog, or bursting into tears in frustration. I began instructing students to "Be gentle on yourself and others in your family through this class."

One of my star student teams was a little toy poodle and her "mom." I could tell the woman worked diligently by how they performed in each class. They excelled. Then one week it was as if they never attended a class before. The dog failed to perform any of his behaviors. He just stopped and looked off into the distance or stared at his owner. When I asked what the problem was, the woman burst into tears.

Her son was seriously ill and because she commuted hours each day to be at his bedside, she no longer had time to train the dog. She felt that the only stable part of her life was her dog training. In a situation where she was helpless to do anything to help her son, her success at dog training gave her something positive to cling to and distracted her from a feeling of powerlessness.

As she sobbed, I reminded her that training was not as important as taking care of her son and herself. The dog helped her feel a sense of normalcy and grounded her, but she attached herself to the outcome and lost sight of what was truly important.

The dog helped her through the current drama, and her temporary dog training failure brought up old issues from her childhood: She felt out of control and thought she was a failure. Control issues often mask abandonment, abuse, or other deep hurts. The loss of control with her dog, her ill son, and her normal life allowed deeper issues that needed healing to emerge. I call this the "hammer-on-the-pushpin" syndrome. Any time the emotional component around an issue is more volatile than the actual incident or issue, the old "stuff" is coming up so it can be released and healed. Eventually, the woman and her dog passed the class with flying colors, and she took time off to deal with her circum-stances and the deeper issues they evoked.

Living by Example

Pets and other animals are examples of how to live by the teachings of the spiritual masters. Animals reflect the teachings of Krishna when they exhibit their ability to live in harmony; they mirror the Buddha's wisdom through their honest actions and compassion; they imitate Christ's example of unconditional love; and, like Sri Ramakrishna, they show unconditional acceptance and connection with all. Because animals possess innate survival instincts, even young animals are adapted for sudden flight-or-fight responses. They adapt to new situations quickly, and they acquire better behavior more rapidly than their human counterparts might expect. New human students marvel at how fast their companion animals respond to training.

Chester was a naughty dog. He ran at, jumped on, and nipped anyone coming to visit. His owners were at a loss over what to do. When I arrived for the consultation, Chester didn't get any great attention for his poor behavior. Instead, he got a fancy dose of behavior modification and quickly learned that to get attention, he needed to sit.

Nancy, his owner, said, "Wow, I can't believe how fast he understood what you wanted." However, as with all new students, animals in school test the parameters. Sometimes they just forget and go back to the entrenched behavior. Chester was no exception and he soon got into trouble; he then made amends. I forgave him as quickly as he forgave me for correcting his poor choice. Nancy didn't understand and asked, "Why are you praising him so quickly?"

Chester received a verbal correction and immediately adjusted his behavior, so he got praise. It is called "being in the moment," and what mattered most was his correct choice and behavior at that instant. He chose proper behavior instead of unacceptable behavior. When Chester tested the parameters, his behavior was more extreme, and so were the corrections. For such infractions, doggie etiquette dictates that canines make amends by licking. I accepted his apology by allowing it. We both forgave each other for any errors, reaching a place of harmony and understanding immediately. Animals teach us to be in the present moment, the only moment.

A lioness guides, teaches, and protects her young. Although she might discipline one of her cubs for a transgression, she quickly forgives and does not hold a grudge. She watches as her offspring struggle with the lessons of life. Those educational experiences mold them and ensure their survival. She understands that schooling is necessary for their growth and success in life. She seldom intervenes, but she does respond to their cries. No matter what their actions, or expressions, she is always nearby in resilient support. Her relationship with her cubs is a reflection of how we should also behave in our relationships, and it parallels our relationship to the Divine.

Animals also are examples of how to move through life peacefully. They conserve their energy for matters of importance. The African lion spends a majority of his time sleeping. The rest of his efforts are focused on hunting or pride interactions.

The African lion reminds us to focus our attention on our relationships, our friends and family. In addition, he is an example of what we need to strive for—being at ease instead of worrying about external circumstances and things beyond our control.

The African lioness does not shy away from tackling other animals who outweigh her. In cases where she is facing an overwhelming situation, she knows others in her support group will come to her aid. They work cooperatively for the good of the pride, or they simply choose another strategy. In some cases, they move on and find a different quarry.

We can learn to take the same attitude as the African lioness when we face overwhelming issues. We can sit back and look at the situation objectively, and commiserate with those who support us. Unbiased opinions during dialogues with those we trust help us find new approaches to solving our problems. Sometimes we don't realize we can just detach and move on.

Although an African lion prefers to avoid a fight, he will bravely face an opponent and his fears. He is aware that it is sometimes necessary to take a stand to protect himself, his territory, or the pride of lions he claims as his family. Even so, he avoids a battle if given the chance, and he picks any skirmishes carefully.

We too must learn to pick and choose our battles. Some situations require that we take a stand and meet our challengers eye to eye, but our biggest demons are those we do not have the courage to face. Often, if we get closer and gaze at them from a new perspective, they end up less overwhelming than we thought. It doesn't matter whether our trials stem from another human being or an internal struggle: When our opponents are confronted, they withdraw under our concentrated focus. A colossal obstacle or problem often turns out to be a manageable situation.

An African lion injured in battle withdraws to lick his wounds, but once the dispute is over, no further energy is given to it. Members of the pride butt heads and rub each other in greeting, cooperative hunting efforts supply a feast, and life goes on. If only we recovered so quickly from our hurts and battles.

If we suffer from an encounter, we too need time to lick our wounds and sort out our priorities and feelings. If we feel wronged, or that we injured another, the best action we can take is to forgive. This forgiveness must be for our choices, our actions, and ourselves, as well as for the target of our hostility, decisions, or conduct. If we don't move on, then we suffer needlessly. One incident illustrates this perfectly; it involved a lion entrenched in his emotions.

The African lion was a beautiful specimen. He had large golden eyes and an amber mane. In his prime, large quantities of testosterone flowed through his veins. I knew trouble was brewing because Champ trudged down the path like a big bully on the warpath. His trainers were inattentive and I could see he was in a mood. He was looking for a fight and we stood directly in his path.

Quickly, I began ordering the group of students under my tutelage into the empty cages around me. I figured Champ would challenge Simba, the other male lion, who had just returned from a long movie shoot. Through an error in judgment, Champ had been displaced and Simba occupied Champ's enclosure. I futilely looked around for some sort of object to place as a visual barrier in front of Simba's cage, but it was too late.

Five hundred pounds of savage beast hauled his trainer down the road and up to Simba. Even though the cage protected the lions from actually getting into a full battle, the altercation was intense. As the trainer stepped up to intervene, Champ followed the chain leash and grabbed him, tossing him into the air like a rag doll. Fortunately, the trainer was not the focus of his attack and Champ turned back to finish his dispute with Simba.

Eventually, we got a truck in between the lion and the injured trainer. We rushed him to the hospital where the doctors assured us he would survive because, by some strange stroke of luck, Champ missed all the vital organs. The students, although a bit shaken, were safe. And Champ was eventually apprehended, but his hostility remained.

The lion bristled at everyone and made no real attempts at friendliness; he never went back to his truly affectionate self. Champ never resolved his territorial issue and his mood got worse over time. I watched sadly as his mental condition deteriorated. Confined to his exhibit, he could no longer be worked safely. This is a good illustration of what can happen when you harbor anger and resentment. Champ's bitterness consumed him and made him mentally ill.

Emotions are powerful. When we harbor anger, resentment, or jealousy, we may feel the power of those emotions, but they are not usually constructive. These feelings need to be resolved before they fester and create larger problems. The inability to forgive or to release volatile feelings only prevents us from moving into a heart-centered equilibrium. Our decisions and actions are more reasonable and successful if we are compassionate and forgive. Some animals are great examples.

Back in the early 1990s, a psychologist friend of mine proposed her theory: Dogs were angels put here on earth to teach us about unconditional love; after all, D-O-G is G-O-D spelled backward. I laughed, but I didn't dismiss the notion. Relationships between dogs and humans contain the amazing capacity to exchange love without restraint. Dogs greet everyone with gusto. They see the best and then translate it through their whole bodies. When greeting their companion, they often run in exuberance, spinning in circles and sometimes barking in excitement. No matter what the owner is like, a dog still loves him or her with all its being. Their actions show unconditional love and they do not harbor any resentment. Dogs forgive and forget quickly.

Humans are more protective of themselves emotionally. Some dogs and other animals find the need to do this, too. Animals with a repeated history of abandonment, or abuse, may start to protect themselves by withdrawing or by exhibiting defensive aggressive behaviors geared toward keeping strangers away. This goes against the true nature of the beast and only contributes to loneliness and isolation. Old emotional wounds must heal so the animal can truly function. This holds true for humans as well.

I first met a dog owner named Warren at a local chili cook-off in the mountains of southern California. Confined to a wheelchair due to injuries sustained in multiple plane crashes, Warren suffered from continuous pain. As a result, he secluded himself in his home and began to drink heavily. The combination of painkillers and alcohol dulled his physical pain but did nothing for his emotional hurt. He didn't go out much and slowly became more and more of a recluse. When things seemed the darkest, he decided to get a puppy.

I befriended Warren as he rolled around the public event escorted by his young Labrador puppy. A multitude of people, especially women, swarmed up and surrounded him. Later, I jokingly commented about how pups were a good way to meet women. He laughed and said, "Jeez, if I knew that before, I would have gotten a puppy a long time ago!" Human perspective changes when animals are involved. People become more accessible with an animal as their shield. Strangers approach others with animals without hesitation. The presence of an animal allows people to feel less vulnerable, less intrusive, and that they share a common interest with the pet owner.

When we have our equilibrium on this rung of the ladder, we naturally become more inquisitive because we experience love, expect love, and feel safe. When we feel secure, we are more affectionate with one another, more compassionate, more passionate about life and others.

Compassion allows us to empathize with others, but it is not the same thing as sympathy. When we are compassionate we take the necessary actions to assist another. Sometimes the only action required is our presence. In other cases, maybe we can help with errands, with meals, or even by our physical presence. Animals intuitively know the right things to do. Therapy animals are known for their skills at gauging the right behaviors for the patient they are visiting.

Joshua was a big brown mutt. He romped with the children in the neighborhood and loved to go for walks with his family. Because he was such a well-behaved critter, he easily earned his "Good Citizen" award. Dogs earn this certificate from the American Kennel Club when they pass a test highlighting certain manners deemed necessary to win the title. Soon, Joshua's owners began exploring other activities for him and got involved in a pet therapy program at a local hospital.

Joshua thrived on the attention. He leaned in quietly when he sat with his elderly patients, and he wiggled enthusiastically with his younger charges. Sometimes his behavior changed and he would quietly lie at the feet of a patient, or near his or her bed. In all those cases, the patients were either recovering from a setback or entering into a critical circumstance. His presence always brought joy and happiness to his charges and something different to talk about. His escapades brought smiles to the staff and patients.

Finding Center Balance on the Pendulum Swing

Mountain lions are naturally curious and playful. When I lived in northern California, it was not uncommon for a mountain lion to trail people during a hike to observe their activities. On the training compound, they bounced excitedly to greet the trainer. Adolescent cats mischievously jumped onto any novice trainer entering their cage. They also liked to launch themselves into the air and spin like a helicopter blade while the trainer clung onto the end of the leash. They expressed their exuberance for life without any reservation.

Our emotions and viewpoints swing from one extreme to the other, and the goal is to find the center balance. Animals reside within the arc of that swing. Although mountain lions can be extremely dangerous, they can also be incredibly affectionate. If a captive cougar feels secure, and considers you part of the family, he chirps at you like a bird. This is a greeting vocalization used to call out to family members. Such behaviors may be mirrored in your own family or in your pets. Some humans lash out verbally, and even physically, when they feel defensive. However, when the home is a safe environment, those behaviors are often replaced by more playful and loving verbal exchanges.

You might hear purrs of contentment from your partner or kids as you snuggle up on the couch. Mountain lions can also purr. That hum is very loud and permeates the surroundings. If you touch the cougar, or if he lies against you, the vibration fills your whole being. If you are heart-centered, then you are able to express your love in a similar way. It wells up in your being until it spills over, touching those close to you and moving out into your community as well.

Usually we can take this energy and share it through the activities we love, as we play with our family and friends. Perhaps you may share it on a large scale by contributing your time to different organizations or charities where you work with others who share the same interests. In any case, when you work through the lessons of the fourth rung, you are ready to move up to the fifth step on the spiritual ladder.

5

Call of the Wolf

The lone howl reverberated through the compound. It was answered first by the other wolves, then by the coyotes, and next by an assortment of animals. In response to the wolf's call, lions, tigers, monkeys, and chimps all joined together in a wild symphony. It lifted in a crescendo and then dropped in a diminuendo. Over my lifetime I have experienced many such concertos orchestrated by wolves. There is something about the call of the wolf that touches a deep chord within me. I always stop what I am doing when the animal choir begins, and sometimes I too even join in and howl.

The subject of myths and mysticism, the wolf is a creature who sparked fear and hatred in the hearts of humans, generated stories and folklore, and ultimately emerged as a resilient icon of our link to nature despite opposition from humankind along the way. The embers of erroneous

> The subject of myths and mysticism, the wolf is clear and direct in its communication. Animals communicate honestly, listen well, give their full attention, don't judge, and are open to whatever comes their way. When we are open to what comes our way, we encounter lessons of truth, honesty, surrender, and the power of the word.

accusations and persecution of wolves have been extinguished and replaced by respect and awe for their virtuous examples of family life and ability for complex communication.

The wolf brings us examples of survival in the wilderness. When alone, a wolf cries for others. The wolf pack bands together as a tight family unit with strong pair bonds that last for life, or until the death of a partner. Hierarchical rules outline roles within the family pack. Wolves work together for the good of the group, providing food and nurturing for the young, sharing babysitting duty, and hunting in cooperation. The adults even give up their food for the young.

Known for their piercing howls, wolves communicate in a variety of other ways. Wolves bark, growl, whimper, cry, and express themselves through posturing and body language. Wolves have diverse expressions. There are low-level threats, when the animal may stand stiffly on its toes, and more intense warnings with a strong eye glare and a toothy sneer. Inviting gestures include a soft gaze, an open-mouthed smile, and a solicitation to play through a bow and a lively bounce. In any case, the wolf is clear and direct in his communication.

Although the phrase "You are behaving like an animal" is not a compliment, it can be, because animals communicate honestly, listen well, give their full attention, don't judge, and are open to whatever comes their way. When we are open to what comes our way on the fifth rung of spiritual development, we encounter lessons of truth, honesty, surrender, and the power of the word.

Tuning In Instead of Tuning Out

Humans are bombarded by external stimuli. Most people are oblivious to the noise level surrounding them. Tuning out, we don't hear the traffic, the buzz of the electric wires, the electronic devices around us, or even the kids. Being disconnected from our surroundings contributes to reasons why many people don't understand animals. We have to learn how to connect and tune in to the real message. Even pet owners do not get proper behavior or cooperation from their animals because they miss the signals. This is why animal training classes are so popular. Humans do not hear or see what animals communicate. This is best illustrated by the more than 4.7 million dog bites that occur each year.

For example, people mistakenly think that a dog wagging her tail is friendly. If they watched the animal closely, they might begin to notice the differences between a friendly dog and an unfriendly dog. A canine who stands up on her toes, exhibits body tension, and displays a stiff tail held high in the air is definitely not friendly. However, a dog with a relaxed body, loose movements, and a happy panting face, combined with a tail wagging back and forth or in a circle, certainly paints a completely different picture.

My most popular class is one in which I teach people how to read animal behavior. I give them tools so they can enhance their animal relationships and begin to understand their pets. These assignments are similar to the ones listed in chapter 8. People who implement the strategies introduced in the course comment on how the class helped them not only with their pets but also with other animals.

Occasionally, I take an animal into "boot camp." My boot camp program is simply a course where the animal comes to live with me and undergoes intensive behavior modification. Such animals have included a dalmatian who bounced off the walls, could never hold still, and whined continuously, as well as dogs who destroyed their environment by chewing or digging or through inappropriate elimination.

When these animals arrive, they receive twenty-four-hour immersion therapy. This rehabilitation work includes socialization with other animals and humans, training for basic obedience, and teaching proper conduct in a variety of environments and settings.

One of my most enjoyable encounters was with a basset hound. Hounds are different animals. Bred for specific traits, hounds are strong-minded and focused. They can also be a bit thick. Gwen was such an animal, her adoptive owners lamented. They insisted their other basset was a gem. The main issue was house-training. Gwen never let them know when she needed to go and was not manageable. So, Gwen came to boot camp.

Gwen was a beautiful creature with big soft brown eyes and black and tan markings on her white fur. When she and my dog met, it was delinquency in the making. They became partners in crime. Imagine my shock when, within half an hour of her arrival, she came up and asked me to let her go out to "do her business." She had other problems, but communicating her need was not one of them.

When I spoke with the owners, they argued in disbelief and asked me to continue my work. Gwen was having a fabulous time with her new human and doggie pals. She enjoyed adventures in the woods, in doggie socials, in school, and at the groomer. However, her owners showed no interest in the changes in her behavior. They clearly did not communicate with the animal—nor did they want to. They paid her tuition but no longer wanted Gwen. As I dialed the rescue organization, it was hard for me to believe the owners didn't care. Fortunately, Gwen did not return home. The agency welcomed her and she went to live with some basset lovers. Gwen left a changed dog, secure, obedient, and with the knowledge of how to communicate more clearly with dense humans.

If people stand back and watch animals, they find an entirely new world opens up. All it takes is the ability to listen, but not just with the ears. Taking in movement, posture, and subtle body cues allows animals to teach observant humans.

Dogs are great animals to start with because there are lots of places to watch them. You can go to a park, for a walk in a neighborhood, to dog shows or classes, or even over to your friend's place. Like us, dogs are communal creatures, so their social nuances play important roles in keeping the peace and getting along.

Dogs have different rituals for greeting. Some include direct approaches; others are indirect. Sniffing and posturing gestures reveal whether the encounter is friendly or antagonistic. Nuzzling and nudging can trigger play or instigate a tense exchange.

Cats, for most people, are more difficult. Small changes in their body tension, eye dilation, or tail movement escalate into a warning bat or bite if a human is distracted. Spectators can glean lots of information quickly because cats show so many behavioral variations during play and other encounters.

Surrendering to the Divine Energy

Animals teach the important concept of willing surrender. When I refused to let students use choke chains in my courses, many people did not understand how to get by without them. Using choke collars is an old-school training method that is still popular today. I prefer other training methods, which involve tools and techniques more palatable to the animal and easier for the layperson to master. Sometimes these other methods take a little longer to obtain the same result, but the attitude of the animal is better.

If you force a dog to sit, you may get the behavior, but the energy behind it is resignation. "Okay, I will do it. Now give me the reward and back off." Or, "Ouch, I'll do that and be done with it, but I am not going to enjoy it." However, if the dog sits because he learned actively, or because he yielded to leadership, the energy behind the behavior is different: "Whatever you want, I will do it." Noting this energy is important because it is also the energy we fight when moving from forcing our personal will to accepting divine will.

If you have ever heard of the "dark night of the soul," I assure you, I've been there. I remember yelling up to the heavens, "What part of 'I can't take any more!' don't you get?" Even though I thought I surrendered, the real concession didn't come until much later. After a tantrum followed by a cry for healing, the energy shifted in a big way. I felt peace and calm replace anger and anguish. Up until then, I remained locked into old behavior and doing what I thought was right. When I gave up and just accepted what was, everything changed.

Pets in training courses do the same thing, but in drastically shorter periods of time. They get the idea right away. I should have paid attention to their example years ago. I certainly noticed it before, but I wasn't quite ready to get the lesson in my own situation. Having clarity sooner would have saved me a lot of grief. My life was shifting into a new direction, but instead of going with the flow, I fought for what I thought I should do and resisted any synchronistic occurrences. If I heeded the examples of my astute canine students, I might have gotten the lesson in eight weeks instead of eight months. Once I opened up to the divine current, my life shifted overnight. I still didn't like some of it, but it definitely got easier.

Embracing Change Positively

Life gets better when we shift away from resistance or negative choices. Negative choices generate lessons, until we learn to make positive ones. Animals show resistance, but they are in touch with what makes life harmonious. When I am teaching a pet, the animal makes poor choices and learns from them, but once the animal makes the correct choice for a positive behavior, he or she gets the message. Occasionally a critter pushes the point, just to make sure.

My favorite example involved a particular dog's humorous lesson about not jumping on people. The dog, Jesse, tested all the parameters. After ignoring the jumping, and then correcting it, Jesse stopped cold. The wheels were turning and he cocked his head. Next, he jumped up and down in the air in front of his owner. He jumped close by, jumped far away, and came back close again.

Next, he jumped and touched one paw on her leg on his way down. Following that, he put his paws up on the table next to her, and so on. Later, during the times when he could not restrain himself, he jumped up and down in front of her. It was amusing, but he didn't jump on her or anyone else again. Humans exhibit this behavior all the time. How many of us will admit that we click the computer mouse, and then when nothing happens, we click again and again? We do that in life, too.

Listening to the Unspoken

Listening is one of the disappearing arts in modern society. Attentive animals do not miss much. Pets pay attention even if you think they do not. When a person is in a dire emotional state, animals use their intuition to listen, to sit close, to be simply in the room, or to act goofy to make the person laugh. They are fully present and available.

"Animal renegades" is the term I give to critters who are very smart or very sensitive and out of control. One such dog, Clyde, was a real pain. He was so naughty his owners did not want to keep him. Unfortunately, they dumped him off in the mountains to survive on his wits. He was rescued, but not before becoming strong-willed and streetwise. Upon arrival at his new home, he promptly terrorized the family's other pets and destroyed the residence. When I got the call for help, I didn't plan to keep him. But three homes later, he had to be rescued from a life on a chain in a litter-filled yard. He was so emotionally distraught that he "anxiety chewed" if left alone for even a minute. And so started our companionship of thirteen years.

Clyde grew into a secure, loyal, and wise companion under my tutelage, and I grew under his. He helped teach other dogs to tolerate other canines; he happily let fearful children and adults approach him; and he enthusiastically educated everyone about how terrific big dogs were. He had a large vocabulary and communicated in subtle ways—he knew what I needed even when I wasn't sure.

When I cried, grew too serious, or became excessively focused on a project, Clyde sensed the need for frivolity. Weighing over one hundred pounds, he flirted with me by displaying a playful bow, highlighted with a rumble so I noticed. If I attempted to ignore him, or told him I was busy, he grabbed a small stuffed animal and romped around the room chomping the toy, sometimes tossing it into the air. He tossed it into my lap, nudged me with it, or in extreme cases dropped onto his back and kicked his legs frantically while he wiggled and juggled the toy between his front paws and mouth. How could I resist?

If I worked too much, Clyde made me move. We sometimes walked for hours, and I never ceased to admire his exuberance for life and the simplest of pleasures, such as my companionship or the thrill of chasing a squirrel in the woods. He often brought to me as a present the biggest rock he could dredge up and carry from the bottom of the lake. When he knew I was distraught, he would lie next to me while I sobbed into his fur. Clyde always listened from his heart and accepted my confidences and me without judging. His happy face and gentle spirit never failed to be there when I needed them. He brought me heartfelt joy.

Clearing through Confession

When people are at their most vulnerable, I see them go to their pets. People cry into their fur; they cling to their bodies; they go outdoors with them; and they pour their deepest, darkest secrets, fears, and transgressions into those soft furry ears. It is truly amazing; their animal companions are their confessors.

Confessions purge us of guilt and negativity. Through the act of confession, people obtain insights and release negative energies. And when people are disillusioned by their religious institutions and leaders, they can still find restitution through God's furry messengers. This is because humans develop deep, trusting bonds with animals and have no reservations about communicating honestly with them. There is comfort in confiding in a furry creature because the animal simply accepts the actions and utterances of the human.

Animals become trusted confessors because they listen well; give their full, undivided attention; and don't judge. They love and accept us and keep delicate declarations confidential. With this comes the comfort of getting something off your chest and the safety of knowing it will go no further.

Unconditional Acceptance

Because animals unconditionally accept their owners or caretakers, they can help with emotional healing. They do not hold grudges and, by refusing to do so, they help us release our judgments of ourselves and others. Sometimes just the example of their unconditional response shifts our energies. In some cases, we can shift an animal's reactions through our example.

When we arrived at the wolf sanctuary, I was wary. There are many facilities that claim to be animal refuges but aren't. Such places are run by charlatans who breed and sell animals and perpetuate a trade that only harms the species to which they swear they are dedicated. In other cases, the places are little better than shantytowns constructed of scraps and crammed with dilapidated animal holding areas. When we entered, relief filled my body as I realized this truly was a wolf sanctuary.

The downside of any public enthrallment with animals is that people attempt to obtain the creatures they so admire. The wolf happens to be one of the more popular animals of our time. Fortunately, it is usually not an easy task to obtain one; regrettably, sometimes a layperson does. Usually the person finds out he or she is unprepared for the unique needs of the animal and the intensive financial and emotional commitment. In the case of the wolf, and the wolf-dog mix, the situation is a nightmare. Few sanctuaries exist to handle the enormous demand for housing and placing these unwanted animals. Only purebred wolves inhabited this particular sanctuary, and despite the fact that the facility was full, three new wolf cubs had arrived shortly before our visit.

After I became acquainted with the staff, we entered into the cub play area. Two inquisitive and outgoing cubs climbed over any solicitous human visitor, but the third skittish cub avoided everyone. I withdrew to sit on a low rock near the middle of the enclosure. While the two cubs played and tormented us, the third cub retreated to the rear and paced. She was clearly uneasy.

The more the other people attempted contact, the more the cub withdrew. However, once the other visitors gave up and turned their attention to the two receptive cubs, the remaining cub decided to approach me. As she advanced, I gently talked to her. She sniffed me and stood nearby. When I simply accepted her presence without physical infringement, she relaxed. Soon, she climbed into my lap and allowed me to cuddle her. I didn't force myself upon her. I just accepted her caution and responded to her overtures. The cub came further and further out of her shell.

The cub's vulnerability mirrored that of some humans. People who feel vulnerable tend to hang back in new situations while they observe from a distance. They wait to see how others behave and then perhaps approach someone who is at ease. Once relaxed, they open up. The cub's interactions also illustrate how a creature will open up when given the opportunity and space to do so. Relaxing and allowing others to move at their own pace encourages growth and forms a solid foundation on which we can build. This acceptance of difference can help us not only in the animal world, but also in our family lives and work environments as well.

After the socializing session with the cubs, I joined the adult wolves. Relaxed and inquisitive, they were not as high-strung as many of the captive wolves I meet. The owner of the sanctuary talked to me about her methods, and she commented on how glad she was to see that the shy cub had shifted. The cub shifted because she was allowed to choose her interactions when she was ready, and not before. Without any judgment or action on my part, she discerned I could be trusted. She felt safe. As a highly sensitive animal, she will have difficulty adjusting to new humans, but at least her new behavior was a start.

Babies and domestic animals greet everyone with the same enthusiasm. Their views are not convoluted by popular opinion, life experiences, or fears. Whereas most people avoid or ignore a homeless person, a baby smiles brightly. A burly man covered with tattoos somehow seems more approachable when holding a small dog. An animal romping at a public beach runs up to greet anyone she meets, regardless of their stature, their clothes, or their nationality. As humans grow older, we become more guarded.

In my experience, discernment is not the same as judgment. Discernment involves making educated decisions based on facts, experiences, and personal values. Judgment usually involves making decisions based on appearances and possibly erroneous information. Avoiding judgments is something I practice. I say "practice" because, despite my not wanting to make them, it happens, and when it does, there is a valuable lesson.

At the height of my domestic animal training career, I taught dog training courses for a variety of private and municipal institutions. My assessments of the dogs and owners were usually pretty accurate, but during one particular session I appraised a woman on how she looked and acted during our first lesson. I pigeonholed her.

Tonya had dark eyes and long black hair and looked as though she had experienced a tough upbringing. Although neat and clean, she appeared to belong in the late 1960s rather than the early 1990s with her long dangly earrings, Native American shirt, jeans, and fringed suede boots. I hate to admit it, but I didn't think she would stay or do the work required. Boy, did she prove me wrong.

After the first session, Tonya shocked me when she shook my hand and thanked me for the lecture. She was at her wit's end with her adopted puppy, Konocti, and my information was something she hoped to find because she didn't want to give up the dog.

At the time, I offered all private and group students the option of attending any of my other series lessons at no charge. They were welcome as long as they did not disturb those with priority enrollment for the particular session. It worked well. To my surprise, Tonya and Konocti came to every lesson, and I ran four to six groups every week. Indeed, Konocti was a very naughty pup. She was headstrong, vocal, nippy, and smart. When she attended puppy socials, she even got into trouble there. In the end, Tonya and Konocti won the class award for "most improved." Tonya worked hard and proved to be one of the most giving and caring people I have met in my life. My initial assessment was wrong; her rough exterior covered a heart of gold. We connected through cooperative behavior and gained a better understanding of each other.

Like the wolf, we strive to connect with families and friends. We band together, form strong bonds, and work toward goals that benefit our kin. We educate and nurture our relations, share caretaking roles, and make sacrifices for our offspring or loved ones. If we have children, they, like the wolf cubs, eventually leave to find life partners, form new families, and define the roles within their own households. Sometimes they are alone for parts of their journey.

There are times in our lives where we may feel alone in the wilderness. We may cover vast territory in the quest to find ourselves, our true values, or our deepest desires. We may also seek the intangible. We may lift our voices and convey joy or distress. Perhaps we simply cry for understanding—or for help. We may feel vulnerable in the wilderness, but it is there that we become clear.

Wolves live in harmony with nature. They adjust to all seasons and take only what they need. In interactions with each other, they articulate clearly, and though there is intensity, there is respect. In one moment, a wolf disciplines another; in the next, he plays. The wolf fully expresses himself distinctly and immediately. Once he's finished communicating, he can move on.

When the wolf snarls and growls, there is a primitive power behind it. Each time I am around a wolf chastising another, I can feel the intensity. I remember a pair of white wolves I once observed. The male was not amiable to people, but the female was very solicitous. The female returned from a walk where she interacted with a human and another wolf. The male was irritable over her absence and disturbed by her interactions. When she returned to the enclosure, he attacked her. The confrontation sounded horrible, but it was ritualistic, not physical. He grabbed her muzzle, stiffly walked around, and growled. In response, she quickly leaned into him and exhibited submissive behaviors, such as licking, whimpering, and wagging her tail. They soon cavorted around the enclosure.

The female wolf was the subject of the discipline, or outburst, and quickly made amends. By "apologizing," the dynamic changed quickly. This wolf illustration is a good example of honesty, surrender, and the power of communication. The male wolf honestly exhibited his true feelings and the intensity behind it, and the female surrendered to the situation, acknowledging his expression. Although humans do not need to be so volatile, they can learn from the wolf's example of true expression and communication.

When people talk about the power of the word, I relate it to the intensity of the wolf's expression. True expression and the power to use our words for good, or for harm, should never be taken for granted. We can gauge our choice of vocabulary and the intensity of our words so they do not harm another. Direct communication and true expression are important, but we, like the wolf, must use restraint.

When we consider our options, how hard is it to say we are sorry? Is it difficult to acknowledge the passionate expressions of the one we hold dear? Do we take the time to listen to the person who needs to dialogue? Do we engage in gossip, or do we honorably engage in a frank discourse? Honest and focused communication presented in a timely manner is an honorable practice.

Tuning In to Nature

When I observe nature, I find many illustrations of how to live my life. Out in the natural world I feel a direct connection with the Divine. Free from distractions, I find myself in a more receptive state. With heightened senses, I do not search and am seldom in expectation, and so I receive answers to my questions.

When physically engaged in the outdoors, I move in synchrony with my surroundings. My concerns fall away as I tune in to nature's broadcast. Gone are my thoughts concerned with daily life and trivial details; instead they are replaced by the sound of waves breaking on the shore, the splash of a goose as she lands upon the lake, and the first insect buzz of the season. I sense the icy winter breeze on my cheeks as the glare of the sun bounces off the surface of the water. The trees rustle as a gust pushes through, and these sensations bring me into the present.

How nice it would be if we all engaged in the sacred art of listening. When you are in conversation with someone else, do you hear what he or she is really saying? Is your mind racing away to ponder your responsibilities? Do you lament over unfinished projects or errands? Maybe you simply wish to be in another location. Instead of really listening, does your mind search for rebuttals to the ideas presented? Or perhaps a question crosses your mind and you interrupt before the speaker is finished? If you answered "yes" to any of these questions, you truly have the opportunity to implement principles taught by the wolf and by nature on this rung of the spiritual ladder. Just listen.

When we are open and receptive, guidance comes, but we need to pay attention. In my life, and in the lives of my friends, messages seem to arrive in groups of three. When three instances reveal the same underlying theme, I consider it guidance, and if I am attentive, I can act on it. Sometimes the same suggestion comes from three different sources. In other cases, I might pick up something on television, encounter it in print, and then hear it from a friend. Impressions or ideas may also come during my meditative prayer sessions; during nature walks; or during less mystical activities, such as driving my truck or washing the dishes. You might receive guidance in similar ways. Pay attention and see where your guidance comes from. Notice when you get impressions, and take notes on how and when you are given suggestions, or how ideas come to you.

When we let go of our expectations and cease to strive for control, we open ourselves up to divine guidance. True, we have to listen and follow the direction given, and we must recognize it. In the case of the wolf, there is a hierarchy of dominance in which there is a definite leader. But although the leader guides the group, he has assistance. He pays attention not only to those around him but also to his surroundings and his instincts. He incorporates his experiences and the lessons from them in his quest for success. His senses are tuned to listen, to watch, and to detect the slightest changes. He may climb to lofty heights to survey his surroundings and get the bigger picture.

If we use the wolf as our example, we learn to open our awareness, pay attention to our senses, and listen to our inner voice. Instead of discounting the direction we receive, we can consciously acknowledge our inclinations or impressions in our quietest moments. With these tools, we leave this rung of the spiritual ladder and climb to the next, where we get a loftier view best illustrated by the eagle.

6

Vision of the Eagle

The eagle careened over my head, diving toward an invisible meal—and taking my breath away in the process. His talons gleamed in the first rays of the sun, and his white head and dark body sharply contrasted against the sky. He missed his target, but quickly adjusted and soared high into the air. As he majestically moved across the ridge, he was highlighted not only in my sight, but also in my mind. In all my years of living in the Big Bear Valley, this was my first glimpse of a wild bald eagle, but it was only the beginning of some unusual and spectacular sightings.

> With eight times the sight ability of humans, the eagle truly has vision. Like the eagle, we can journey to new heights and look back upon our lives, our actions, and the challenges we encounter. From this elevated view, we gain a different perspective and obtain the clarity of distance.

Bald eagles are enormous birds. Weighing up to fourteen pounds, with a wingspan of six to seven feet, these birds roost on snags or dead-topped trees. Their sheer size requires tremendous energy and space for takeoff and landing. Treetop perches provide the birds with roosting spots and favorable hunting views. They react to the slightest disturbances and can see the smallest speck in full and clear detail. Eagles are highly attuned to receive information and are sensitive to their surroundings.

Although Native American legends and symbolisms of this bird vary, a Pueblo Indian legend explains that prayers and messages are sent to the eagles because they represent the link to the divine Spirit. Because they rise on wind currents, and swirl upward out of sight, they are known as winged messengers to the Creator. As they vanish from view, they remind us to move upward, and they also help lift us up to the next rung of the spiritual ladder.

On the sixth rung, the eagle brings us lessons on how to develop farsightedness, the ability to detach and observe, and the discernment to know when to participate and when to change our views and let go. Eagles demonstrate how to take advantage of arising opportunities and how to recover from adversity. In addition, they illustrate how to delve into new waters, grasp what is needed, and emerge with new sustenance.

With eight times the sight ability of humans, the eagle truly has vision. Like the eagle, we can journey to new heights and look back upon our lives, our actions, and the challenges we encounter. From this elevated view, we gain a different perspective and obtain the clarity of distance. With clarity comes the ability to see the options and opportunities we miss when we are too close to a situation. We truly do have a choice in how we move through life, but to move forward adeptly, we must see clearly. We also need to let go.

Letting go of ideas or patterns we still cling to after long periods of time is difficult, but it is necessary for progress and health. If a captive bird is not given a variety of perches to climb and grip, then it develops problems and loses fitness. We also need to detach and move around to another perch. It is essential to delve into our dreams, desires, and motivations to see whether we have deviated from our flight path and lost our way.

Eagles are survivors. At one time, pesticides and persecution drove these creatures to the brink of extinction in some areas, but now they have recovered. These eagles survived daunting challenges. They adapted and improved and are examples of how we can also overcome discouraging setbacks.

Although we can surmount our challenges alone, sometimes help comes from unforeseen sources. In the case of the eagle, humans created the problems, but were also responsible for fixing them. Detrimental pesticides were banned, and eagle fans worked hard to get legislation to protect the birds and their habitats. In our own situations, help might come from people we know, but it can also come from avenues we never expected, and from people we never imagined. In other instances, a sudden insight might reveal a solution, or we may experience divine inspiration or direction.

There was a time when I desperately needed guidance and it finally came after diligently looking within. While employed in a good management job at an oceanarium, I applied for admission to an elite college program. Within a short period of time, I became very ill, lost my job, lost my apartment, and was not accepted into the college program I desperately desired. While the doctors attempted to diagnose the problem, I moved to northern California and spent time in nature and in alternative health therapies. I was at a loss as to what I should do, since all my plans seemed ruined. Then one day as I sat in quiet contemplation, I experienced an epiphany. I realized I could move and gain more experience and try again. Shortly after, my health shifted and I returned to southern California. I worked to gain more animal experience and secured entry into the illustrious program. The guidance came suddenly and clearly. When I followed that direction, all the doors opened up to allow me to pursue it.

Like the eagle, I was an opportunist. Eagles watch and recognize signs of the times. Eagles are scavengers and predators. They struggle to survive but also cull the weak and sick. Their example does not mean taking advantage of others, or harming them, but instead grasping prospects that benefit us, our families, and our communities. What the eagle exemplifies in this instance is the practice of paying attention to our surroundings and being alert to new opportunities. Like the eagle with his talons targeted toward his prey, we should seize the opportunities within our grasp. When the opportunity arises, the eagle might seize a fish from the clutches of another eagle, or steal it from another predator. Eagles grasp tightly in some cases, and in others they let go and move on to another pursuit.

Eagles also know when the seasons change and it is time to leave. They take full advantage of the opportunities that such travels yield and revisit favorable areas. How many of us fail to recognize when we have outgrown a situation, or when it is not in our best interest to remain in a harsh environment? Like the eagle, we must recognize when a place no longer yields what we need to remain healthy and happy.

Donna was unhappy. She had left a good animal management position to join up with a new man and what she believed was an innovative bird program. She relocated across the United States; expanded her expertise by learning how to raise baby birds; and began to do educational programs, write, and produce bird-related products. The potential was there, but she found her new environment frustrating and unsupportive. Although she gained valuable skills and contacts, she missed her friends and family. Ultimately, she decided it was best to leave the situation. Soon her life was on a different course, where she was supported by those close to her and happily involved in more positive environments.

The eagle encourages us to dive into new waters with conviction. If we penetrate beyond the surface into the depths of our emotion and creativity, we too can grasp what is needed and emerge cleansed, with new tools and energy obtained through our efforts. We have to be willing to dive. Venturing into new realms is possible even when we cannot see beyond the exterior; we just have to commit and trust we will emerge safely.

Using Our Own Intuitive Gifts

Animals depend on their senses to survive. Vision is not always the primary sense—intuition may be. The sixth rung of growth is about tapping into your intuitive sense without getting muddled by external situations.

If you watch animals in motion, you begin to notice how they integrate into their environment. Herd animals are highly attuned to each other and to the predators around them. When at ease, they munch and go about their normal activities. When they intuit that something is amiss, the atmosphere changes. There is an electrical charge or tension in the air, other animals may become quiet, and then it seems like an explosion when the animals suddenly react by fleeing the area, bounding off in unison.

Although all animals are highly attuned to their surroundings and the events occurring within close proximity, there is a serenity around pelicans. Pelicans demonstrate how we can work in harmony to achieve goals beneficial to all. They work together to benefit the group and gain time for other endeavors. In addition, they illustrate how it is possible to keep a calm demeanor when working frantically in other areas of life. Watchful with focused vision, they pay attention not only to what is going on around them but also to what is going on underneath it all.

White pelicans arrive in huge flocks, with hundreds, and sometimes thousands, of majestic birds riding the wind currents and gliding in unison. They swirl in an aerial ballet until they pick a spot to land on the water. Once on the surface, they cooperatively hunt. Although they appear calm and collected above the surface, their submerged feet move energetically, propelling them forward in an arc while they herd fish into the shallows. The fish can then be scooped up into the large pouches of their beaks, in the same way fishermen use nets. Their cooperative efforts ensure success. Cooperation also allows them to engage in other less strenuous but vital behaviors, such as sunbathing and preening. Their collaboration is beneficial, but their movements are also guided by an intuitive sense.

How do animals know when their owners are on their way home or when an excursion is imminent? Part of this knowing is associated with human behavioral patterns, key phrases, or time-linked triggers. However, animals use a different sensory perception.

Habits and phrases activate behavioral responses in animals. Most behavior problems, such as "separation anxiety," can be traced back to owner activities. In most cases, humans unwittingly trigger and escalate stress situations, and then accidentally reinforce the inappropriate behavior.

Dena described how her dog became panicky after an earthquake and the resulting aftershock tremors. She quickly called me for help. During our phone consultation, she revealed her attempts to comfort the dog. I suggested she stop consoling him because it only reinforced the fearful response. She took the advice and within twenty-four hours the dog no longer shook or acted fearful. This same type of overly consoling attention creates problems for animals when their owners leave and arrive.

When Clyde first arrived at my home, he anxiously chewed when left alone for even brief amounts of time. After behavioral therapy, my comings and goings were no longer a big deal. No time-linked triggers existed to help him guesstimate when I might return home or when he might travel with me, nor were there any other regular patterns to elicit suspicions of when I might leave or arrive. Even so, every time I arrived home from a trip, he sensed it in advance and was always wait-ing. Numerous pet owners can attest to the same behavior.

When Bea's dog disappeared, she intuited something horrible had happened. For the next forty-eight hours she searched for him. In her search efforts she took long walks around the area and was drawn toward a road near a dry lakebed. There she spotted her dog. He lifted his head to catch her attention. Severely injured, he was rushed to surgery and sur-vived. How did she find him? She followed her inner sight. Many moth-ers attest to the fact that they sense when their children are in danger.

We all have inner sight and sense, but how often do we dismiss it? The little things, such as following hunches and having them turn out right, thinking about someone and then having him or her appear, or calling friends and having them exclaim, "I was just thinking about you" are intuitive connections and part of a larger vision. Try the fol-lowing exercise and see what happens.

Take a jaunt to a local park, zoo, or wilderness area. Next, pick any type of animal or bird close by and gaze at it intensely. See how long it takes for the animal to turn around and look at you or fly away. If you are staring at a domestic animal, the animal may approach you. In most cases, it won't take very long. Intuitively, the animal picks up on the energy focused on it. Many prey species ignore predators until a hunt is in progress. Their inner vision makes them alert.

Today, many of us seek to connect with this intuitive power. However, the easy road is not the answer. Those seeking guidance from spiritual counselors, psychics, and others miss the point. We need to look within and use our own sight, a divine gift of inner vision, instead of becoming adult dependents or spiritual junkies. Prophecy, or the gift of sight, is not a bad talent, but using outside assistance as a crutch hampers your personal spiritual progression.

Most good animal people I know are intuitive. That is the differ-ence between those with talent and those who just get by. Anyone can learn techniques, but to excel, you must use your instincts. Over the years, one of my main goals has been to teach people how to understand their animals. It is important for pet owners to learn how to use their own intuitive gifts to connect with their animals. When my students ask me for an answer, I reply, "What do you think?" or "What do you see?" At first, this might meet with resistance because they don't trust their abilities. Soon, they begin to grasp the subtle clues and hunches and this helps them progress quickly.

When questions arise in group animal-training situations, I ask all participants to share their insights. People share what they suspect, feel, or see, and then others begin to recognize the same things, gain more confidence, and awaken their latent abilities. The more students practice, the more information they receive. This empowers them in relation to their animals and also helps them with other creatures.

Sydney brought her dog, Sampson, a sturdy boxer, to class because she did not understand him, nor did she have any control over him. He was friendly, but he had learned to get his way by pushing his weight around. In her constant struggle to control him, Sydney continuously chattered and distracted the entire class. I offered to use Sampson as a demonstration animal for the session, and within minutes he stood quietly. When I asked the class to explain why this had happened, they were initially perplexed. I handed Sampson back to his owner and everyone watched as he resumed his hyperactive behavior. This time I coached Sydney about different techniques regarding the leash, conscious movement, and communication. Within a short amount of time the dynamic shifted. I took Sampson, worked with him, and again asked the class to explain the difference. Among an assortment of behaviors, the students noticed that I used purposeful movement, that the dog learned to follow instead of lead, and that my communication was immediate and clear. Sydney managed to get a good start on recognizing what worked and practiced the techniques during the session. By the next class she had better skills, and by the end of the course, she owned a well-behaved dog and knew how to deal with other canines effectively. She claimed her walks became "hassle free" because she knew not only how to manage Sampson but also how to deal with any unsupervised mutts that bothered her. She learned to trust herself.

It is important to learn to trust yourself rather than rely on the guidance of someone else, which brings up an important point. When I started my career in the 1970s, animal psychics were rare. In fact, people with the gifts of clairaudience or clairvoyance were suspected of malevolence. Today it is common to hear about psychic networks, psychic fairs, and televised shows featuring psychics. One popular show involves an individual working to communicate the innermost thoughts and desires of animals to their pet owners.

Although we should use any avenues that can assist us, they should not become crutches. We need to do our own work and strive for development. Placing our trust in our higher power is one thing. Putting it outside of ourselves and into the hands of someone else is never a good idea because it is disempowering. We are meant to learn how to connect with our animals ourselves. Our ancestors took the time to connect and knew animals and their patterns intimately. We, too, have those same abilities and should spend our efforts there rather than spending our dollars on someone else's efforts for us.

While I was affiliated with an innovative animal clinic in San Diego county, my colleagues and I familiarized ourselves with the techniques and practices each of us used. When I arrived with my pets for the communication session with my associate, I already had a good sense of my animals and their needs, but I found the course very revealing. I enjoyed connecting with the pets I had just met, obtaining information from them, and getting immediate confirmation about the accuracy of that information from the pet owners present.

Again, there is nothing wrong with getting help when you need it. I selectively consult with other animal behaviorists and experts on specific cases and have worked with three well-known animal psychics. In my search for the best methods, I also explore alternative therapies to address animal issues. One unusual animal case involved a kinkajou (a rainforest cousin of the raccoon, popularly called a honey-bear), who had suddenly attacked his handler. Without divulging any details of the case to the psychic, I submitted the animal's photo. During the session the kinkajou told the communicator that his owner was upset about the attack. The kinkajou made it clear that he didn't want to talk about it, but he complained about the other kinkajous receiving more attention, and that he felt ill.

There is a time and a place to seek help. If you decide to hire someone, regardless of his or her profession, use discernment and make sure the person is a well-established and trustworthy professional.

Focusing on Our Inner Sight

Eagles glide gracefully on the currents. They literally get high, but not in the sense that some humans do. Tapping into our sacred selves does not include the abuse of drugs and alcohol. Legal or not, these substances form barriers to our inner knowledge. In our society, there is wide use and acceptance of pharmacology. People talk about their prescriptions as freely as they do a sporting event. Perhaps this is progress, but even our children take drugs at young ages for issues that might be symptoms of something else gone awry. Abuse of drugs of any kind tend to mask our feelings and cloud our inner sight.

Meditation, prayer, chanting, yoga, and other practices can connect a person to the Divine, but some people want to shortcut the process. These people use drugs, such as peyote or marijuana, to connect to spirit. When I studied alternative healing practices, I was alerted to how these actions can create holes in the auric field, the energy field of the body, and open up a person not only to the Divine but also to negativity.

Alas, we are impatient. In our daily lives we expect instant gratification. We have the instant connections through the Internet and cell phones, and we no longer want to wait. Even our restaurants cater to a fast-paced lifestyle. There is no fast track to connecting with the Divine, but that doesn't prevent people from trying. Drugs, pharmaceutical or otherwise, have become common options for numbing our pain or burying inconvenient issues. Dis-ease is commonplace. Substances allow us to function but squelch the cries of our spirits. Drugs may simply mask the symptoms of underlying unrest and dull our senses. These senses include instincts that move us forward into spiritual growth and deeper insights.

Animals survive on their wits. They cannot afford altered senses, because that state could be fatal. Animals must be in the moment and deal with whatever is presented. If their natural life is infringed upon by humans, complications occur. Not too long ago I worked at a very large zoo. When the head behaviorist suggested using Prozac on the animals to calm them, I was appalled.

Wild animals have different reactions to drugs than domestic animals do, and although there are appropriate uses for pharmacological drugs within the domestic animal behavior modification field, side effects are a risk. It seemed premature to request drug intervention before making a proper determination of what the cause of the stress was.

Due to public and financial pressures to open the exhibit, the animals had not been given adequate time to acclimate. Complicating matters further was the fact that the animals were not properly introduced to each other prior to integration. Finally, altercations occurred during competition over inaccurately placed feeding and enrichment devices (such as random food dispensers and toys), and stress levels escalated because of them. Zoo management seemed more eager to head for a quick fix rather than work to solve the underlying issues. The animals needed time to settle in graciously instead of being pushed forward quickly to satisfy the humans involved with the project.

Along with pharmaceuticals, there are other crutches that are deemed acceptable in modern life. For instance, some people spend years and years in the same seat, at the same time, chatting with the same therapist without becoming enabled or empowered. Counseling, support groups, and therapy are great tools and benefit many individuals, but refusing to move into self-empowerment and self-reliance is crippling. We must be willing to be uncomfortable. As we move through the discomfort, we learn and grow, and our overwhelming issues lose their power over us. That is how we move up the rungs of the ladder—we grab one rung and pull ourselves up, then lift our feet to the next rung as well. It is the climb that gets us to the top. We don't need the crutches; we need to do the work. Tools can be like elevators: they can accelerate our upward journey, but they are useless when there is no power. By relying on external power, we lose our fitness.

Instead of seeking answers elsewhere, let's spend more time with our animals and ourselves. We can grasp simple lessons and insights by just being present with the creatures close to us. Animal vision is better than television. This is also a dynamic process, where the animal looks deep into the depths of our being and sees the best we have to offer. It is not a passive process; it is an active one. In our relationships, we both grow and learn from each other. We need this exchange to be clear. Our wits need to be sharp and accessible.

Entering the Universal Flow

I watch animals constantly. When I look at the pelican, I see black and white wings. Those markings are striking, but when I watch the birds work those wings, negotiating the currents, squabbling for space, and other such activities, I am reminded that the world around me is really not black and white. Life has many shades. Sometimes the contrast allows us to see other options.

Sometimes, the black and white dissolves into a gray mist that edges over the water. When the mist engulfs everything, and I lose sight of the separation, I wonder whether it is a symbol of immersion or integration. There is an ebb and a flow involved in uniting with nature and in connecting with Spirit. This process is not always easily grasped.

In response to the human quest for connection to spirit and nature, many seminars and trendy programs promise to facilitate that union. Unfortunately, the focus of many of these programs is on the external instead of the internal. When a Native American author was a guest at my writing group, she shared a wealth of personal experiences and humor. As she talked about people who imitated the Native American path, she pointed out that they had no true connection with it. They simply were not Native American and, no matter how hard they tried, following that road was not appropriate. As she shared stories about "spiritual junkies," we all laughed in understanding and discomfort, mainly because we all knew similar stories and many in the group had embarked on comparable quests.

During the session, I remembered a paper my teacher gave me when I finished my master's level of Reiki training, an alternative energy healing practice. Attached to my diploma was a cartoon depicting a person with all the latest "toys" related to spiritual healing and growth. The caricature showed crystals, ear cones, colored goggles to balance the energy centers, a guardian angel, an aura-amplifier backpack, reflexology sandals, Tarot cards, a stack of books with trendy titles, geomagnetic protective underwear, and other piles of gadgets and aids popular today. It was a humorous reminder for me to stay centered and not to look for external sources of connection.

When my attention returned to the writing group, I was glad to hear our speaker summarize what is important: "Be who you are rather than a wanna-be." In other words, find a practice within your culture and time and claim it. Animals teach us how to be authentic. They are genuine in every way and each one is unique.

The bat, with close to a thousand different species, is an intriguing animal. And although some people find the bat enthralling, others find it horrific. But any way you perceive it, the bat is a distinctive creature and the only mammal that truly flies. Bats are specially adapted.

Bats illustrate the advantage of being flexible. Their thin elastic wing membranes are fashioned from skin. Their arms and long digits form the upper skeletal frame of the wings, while their legs and feet anchor their posterior. Known for hanging upside down from the tops of caves and from branches or foliage, they amble about with great dexterity. If we imitate the example of the bat, we can turn things upside down, obtaining a unique perspective that allows us to literally stretch our wings as we venture over new territory.

Bats are very adept in the air and rely on echolocation to navigate. To use echolocation, the bat emits sounds (above the range of human hearing) that bounce back as echoes. This allows bats to guide themselves in flight and to locate prey. Even though bats do use their other senses, these mammals listen for guidance with their large ears instead of relying on what can be seen. We, too, should listen, not only to others but also to the inner voice that guides us in the same manner that echolocation guides the bat. We need to learn to rely on different types of guidance and be open to the divine inspiration that enters into our perception when we are truly listening.

Although bats live in a variety of environments, most people think of bats as living in caves. Anywhere bats congregate, there are large piles of guano. These deposits, rich in nutrients, pile up high and can be used to provide nourishment vital for plant growth. The lesson here is that although we might think our lives are piled high with excrement, we can always make fertilizer out of it!

Mindfulness Matters

When we observe our animal brethren, it becomes apparent that they spend lots of time hunting, nurturing their young, guarding their territories, and caring for themselves. However, animals also engage in quiet time.

One of the practices animals have mastered is meditative focus. And I don't mean sitting and contemplating. Animals stay in the present moment in whatever they do. Sometimes they sleep, but meditative times happen in a constant stream. There are more meditative activities, such as relaxing in the sun, in the shade on the grass, or under a tree taking in the scenery, but it is also how animals live life every moment. Prayer and meditation can occur throughout your day. If every human spent as much time in meditation as animals do, our world would be transformed.

The Vietnamese Buddhist monk, Thich Nhat Hanh, is best known for his teachings about meditative mindfulness. His teachings are simply to be where you are and notice what you are doing in that moment. He teaches what the animals show us. In one of his examples he discusses chores. If you wash dishes, then you should focus on washing the dishes. Don't think about what you are going to do next, don't hurry, simply focus on washing the dishes, notice your activity, and do the best you can in that moment.

In contrast to animals, we occupy ourselves with constant activity and noise. Television, radio, and cell phones are big distractions. Fitness clubs, nightclubs, sports events, concerts, and similar activities are others. If you don't think this is so, take a note pad with you and jot down your activities for one day. Most people don't know how to truly relax.

Even though I live above an eagle sanctuary and adjacent to a lake, many of my visitors don't take the time to notice either one. Most visitors come up to the mountains and keep busy to have fun. Many blare their radios instead of switching them off and allowing the sounds of nature to seep in. My friends from the city often complain about how quiet it is.

In contrast to their complaints, I find it noisy with all the birds, bugs, and sounds of the wind through the trees and other plant life. At night, the coyotes hold raucous conventions and the raccoons pillage boisterously through the neighborhood. In the morning, I wake up to the hammering of the local flickers. I never find my surroundings to be silent. In contrast, when I venture to the city the escalated noise levels are a shock to my system. Other jolts include the differences I find in people's priorities about what is important.

Many humans place more value on the tangible and the material, but getting to the place where we value who we are and how much we have grown is ultimately worth more. Animals see us with pure vision. A puppy will run up to charm anyone. She sees all people as worthy of attention and love. When we can get to the point where we have that sight, then we have accomplished something. Gaining this new perspective can be an interesting process, because we get too used to moving along in our lives in the same manner.

This experience was brought home to me one morning while on a walk with my dog. Although we often hiked in the forest, I didn't always see the things he took pleasure in. On this particular morning, after a good snowfall, we headed to the nearby meadow. During the hike, I watched him dart back and forth. Before the snow covered the ground, I knew he was scenting, but that day the tracks were revealed for me to see and follow. Paw prints were everywhere, left by rabbits, squirrels, a coyote, and other dogs and cats from the neighborhood. My eyes were opened to the normally unseen. What I had taken on faith was revealed.

My senses also heightened, so I heard the crackling of the ice in the sun, the drops hitting the carpet of snow below, and the soft thuds of the clumps dislodging from the tree boughs. My perspective broadened and I shared my dog's excitement as I followed the tracks with him. The simple sighting of those prints symbolized a new vision for me.

If we learn to claim the lessons on the sixth rung of the spiritual ladder, we begin to incorporate the examples the animals of flight give us. We pay attention to our intuition and our dreams; we spread our wings to explore new territories. When we get to the place where we attain this new perspective, we are ready for the seventh rung, where we expand our minds and learn from the example of the dolphin.

7

Mind of the Dolphin

Early mornings on the ocean speak to my soul. When out on the sea, I connect with a deep sense of calm and quiet expectation. Perhaps that is why water symbolizes the subconscious or deeper levels of the mind, as well as emotions. On this particular morning the water was calm and I quickly spotted whale footprints: large impressions on the surface of the water made by the tail flukes of a whale as it dived. This was a good sign, and we quickly picked up the trail of several leviathans. The whales surfaced and traveled in a relaxed formation; one breached over and over again, leaping high out of the water and then returning to the marine environment with a large splash. So far it had been an exceptional whale watch, because we had witnessed an assortment of behaviors and many different whales.

> Dolphins represent the ultimate connection with the Divine. We glimpse harmony, synchronicity, and the importance of breathing. We must find the equilibrium within our lives, take care of our needs, cooperate with those in our inner circle, and find time to interact in ways that lift us up.

The face of the ocean was smooth, and the only breeze was the one created by the forward movement of the boat as we pulled away from the group of whales. As the morning blanket of fog was chased away by the early afternoon sun, the surface of the water glimmered like diamonds, and a new buzz of excitement quickly spread through the onlookers.

As I gazed out toward the horizon, a large school of dolphins raced toward the boat. The dolphins undulated in and out of the water in small clusters, and there were hundreds of them. The small black, gray, yellow, and white cetaceans were common dolphins. As they fell into line with the boat, the gasps and squeals of surprise began to rise from the people on board. The cries of delight announced each time a dolphin broke away from the pod, swimming swiftly just under the surface at the bow of the boat, until it catapulted up into the air. Each person on board got a good glimpse of a glistening, streamlined dolphin body. Like the legends of old, the animals led the way into the seemingly uncharted waters, and only when we approached the shallower waters of the island did they head off for different pursuits.

Dolphins, especially the bottlenose species, capture the imagination and hearts of almost everyone. Popularized in the 1960s by the television character known simply as Flipper, these animals create an excitement like no other. Their perpetual smile, gregarious nature, and incredible intelligence lure us closer. Humans retell the myths about this animal and ponder the many tales arising from our fascination with this creature.

Dolphins represent the ultimate connection with the Divine and help us with lessons on the seventh rung of the spiritual ladder. From this high perch, we glimpse harmony, synchronicity, and the importance of breathing. Dolphins illustrate the importance of adapting and demonstrate the ability to exist in a different dimension. Just looking at a dolphin reveals a wealth of information.

Although they breathe the same air we do, they are suspended in an environment that requires attunement to every aspect of survival.

Dolphins adapted to their surroundings by developing large brains and sleek bodies. Their heightened senses reveal information through vibration, intention, and echolocation. These cetaceans can travel to great depths and withstand the pressure. They know how to adapt to their changing environment, and they illustrate the importance of conscious breathing. Efficient in their efforts, they navigate swiftly when needed, but dolphins always find time to frolic and play.

Their sleek and strong bodies are perfect for moving through their aquatic atmosphere and demonstrate that when we streamline our lives, things go easier for us as well. If we are strong in body and mind, we feel better and are more efficient. Our lives move smoothly when we fine-tune ourselves to cope with the challenges we encounter. We must find the equilibrium within our lives, take care of our needs, cooperate with those in our inner circle, and find time to interact in ways that lift us up.

My first close encounters with dolphins started at Marineland of the Pacific in Palos Verdes, California. One of the earliest facilities of its kind, this oceanarium was created in the mid-1950s and was managed by a handful of scientists. The animals housed there included sea turtles, fish, eels, sharks, rays, and sea mammals. Sea life filled the aquariums and the minds of children and adults, and many people learned for the first time that dolphins and whales were not fish, but mammals.

The dolphin's capacity for intelligence and development began to be recognized in the public realm during the mid-1940s. Florida's Marineland curator Arthur McBride and McGill University psychologist Donald O. Hebb noted the mammal's large brain and described their observations regarding its emotional and behavioral traits in captivity. Subsequent studies and research suggest the size of the dolphin brain correlates with some of its unique adaptations for deciphering information from the environment.

The melon, the popular name for the dolphin's smooth bulbous forehead, is one of those unique adaptations. It helps the animal attain clarity when things get murky; it acts as an acoustic lens. The dolphin can obtain a three-dimensional picture by sending out echolocation clicks through the melon. These sound waves bounce back and are then transmitted along the lower jaw, where they eventually give the dolphin information he or she can process.

Always gathering information, dolphins are inquisitive animals. When we worked below the dolphin arena tank, the dolphins clicked and whistled at us while we worked. They would hang motionless in the water observing us, surfacing only for a breath, and resubmerging to continue their scrutiny.

If, like the dolphins, we use our brain power, we can begin to see all the different aspects of situations and people we encounter. Although we don't use the same type of sonar to achieve clarity, we can home in to get a clearer picture by doing some investigation or by engaging in detached observation. We, too, can benefit from the information coming from an inner voice or the inner vision attuned to messages originating from a higher source.

It is usually when I am out in nature or occupied with some routine task that I receive helpful information. Ideas or answers to difficult questions seem to pop into my head. In some cases, I consciously ask the question and wait for an answer to appear. Many friends tell me it is because my sonar is out there working. The waves go out and bounce back with information, and that inner voice can be heard when my brain is not actively engaged in running thoughts through my head.

Many spiritual practices are geared toward facilitating this process: Quiet prayer encourages us to reach out to the Divine; repetitive chanting or focused movement provides a focal point for the mind; contemplation or meditation encourages the process of clearing the mind and teaches receptivity.

Although I work at constant prayer and engage in meditative practices, I feel my best when I am out in the natural world or with animals. My spiritual practice of choice involves walking in nature, and for me it works in the same manner as some of the more popular spiritual practices.

Moving in Harmony

Dolphins have highly developed senses. If you watch a herd of these animals, you can see they move in synchrony. They undulate in unison, turning and changing their speed together. They align with each other, and the group benefits from the arrangement. Dolphins intuitively move in harmony, and in some cases they engage in altruistic behavior by helping others, even those of a different species. This is not to say that animals always live their lives as the best examples, for they too have shortcomings. There are stories of transmutations from dolphin to human and vice versa, and the most popular dolphin tales are those where dolphins have assisted humans. However, there are other less happy outcomes from human-dolphin interactions, too.

Many years ago, a cetacean researcher from England documented some of the most popular dolphin stories. She researched stories of solitary dolphins interacting with humans in the waters near New Zealand, Florida, South Carolina, Costa Rica, Italy, England, Wales, Spain, Ireland, France, Scotland, and the Bahamas. One of the more popular animals was a creature who initially patrolled the harbor and chased boats.

In the summer of 1955, a female bottlenose dolphin swam into Hokianga Harbor on the west coast of Auckland, New Zealand. Opononi was a friendly dolphin and developed a special relationship with a young girl, towing her around the bay. Soon, thousands of visitors started to arrive to visit this friendly dolphin and locals began to fear for Opo's safety. Shortly after the government passed a law limiting human interaction with her, she was found dead. After a public funeral, a statue of Opo was erected in commemoration of her unique spirit.

Dolphin group interactions are also common in Australia. Accounts involve not only bottlenose dolphins but also transient orcas, who were known for their efforts in helping human whaling back in the 1800s. The pod symbiotically assisted whalers by chasing down the quarry. Perhaps the most popular citation involves the dolphins of Monkey Mia, a small site located in Shark Bay.

The Shark Bay region is recognized for its unique marine environment and aquatic life. Dolphins seeking interactions with humans in this area of Australia were first noted in the 1960s. At least three generations of wild bottlenose dolphins have made a ritual of visiting this small beach north of Perth. Holeyfin was one of the more well-known resident females. Named for the hole in her dorsal fin, she is thought to have lived in the Monkey Mia area since the 1970s, and possibly earlier. This dolphin was involved in some interesting dolphin behavior discoveries; when she died in 1995, tooth analysis revealed her to be about thirty-five years old.

Presently, small groups of dolphins visit the beach at Monkey Mia each morning to interact with visitors, who can walk among them in the shallows. For safety reasons, this event is now under the supervision of full-time national park rangers. In other areas of the beach, visitors swim and observe dolphin antics and natural interactions. We still have a lot to learn about these creatures, and since the early 1980s Monkey Mia has become one of the most important dolphin research centers in the world. Scientists conduct ongoing studies involving the dolphins who visit the beach and the offshore population of dolphins in the area.

Although many of the social encounter stories recount friendly interludes, such as dolphins towing swimmers holding onto their dorsal fins, pushing people toward shore, and other activities that include playing with and even riding on the back of a dolphin, there are examples that are not so positive. There are instances where dolphins have pinned divers at the bottom of the seabed, pushed swimmers and surfers out to sea and then prevented them from swimming ashore, and even rammed swimmers and smashed surfboards. When we observe animals, we must admit that, although they can illustrate ideal qualities and examples of spiritual lessons, they also can show us negative lessons and teach us to use care in our interactions.

Dolphins illustrate how to pay attention to those close to us and work toward harmonious activities rather than toward our own selfish desires or needs. When we work in harmony, all benefit. Groups of dolphins move in unison, traveling in formation and working together during hunts.

If we move in conjunction with life's events, we follow the path to a more harmonious life. When we move outside ourselves into bigger goals or projects, we grow and expand. Selfless behavior ignites the spirit of compassion and goodwill in others and takes it forward into the world. Eventually, it moves others into a more harmonious space.

Dolphins also move with intention and direction. They navigate swiftly and take advantage of opportunities that arise. Many dolphins leap at the chance to ride the bow of a boat to accelerate their journey. Others might simply take a break to enjoy the ride.

Whatever the case, dolphins illustrate how we humans can move ahead with intensity. We can choose to move forward on our own volition, or we can find unique breaks where we can enjoy ourselves in the process, making our advances effortless.

Making Time to Play

Even though life in the ocean, or as a performer, can be challenging, dolphins always find time to frolic and play. In my early days at Marineland, my dolphin pals continually demanded attention. There was a holding pool in an area of the park where the public did not spend a lot of time. When anyone walked by, the dolphins would propel the upper half of their bodies up out of the water so they could see above the edge of the tank, and then bob back down again in a behavior called a "spy-hop." This gave them a good view of who might be in close proximity.

On most days, I took my breaks in that area so I could spend time with the dolphins, but sometimes I scurried by on the way to my next assignment. More often than not, if the dolphins saw me, a large brightly colored ball hurled out of the tank toward me in an effort to encourage me to play. Any volleys done with their tail flukes were amazingly accurate.

The dolphins lured me into a few minutes of pleasure and laughter even on hectic days. This behavior is true for both young and old animals of all species. They get humans to lighten up and play. When a human is distracted, many animals encourage, even demand, that the person come back to the present and pay attention. They are our anchors to our true selves and to what is important.

An acquaintance of mine named Elizabeth was a self-employed workaholic. She would go to her office and then come home and log onto the computer to work some more. Meals were usually eaten at the desk and the only change in her schedule occurred during the weekend, when she did not visit the office. Instead she ran errands, but she still worked diligently at home.

Kitty Flora arrived unexpectedly one evening when Elizabeth was taking out the trash. "There she was, this scrawny little cat, foraging around the dumpster. I just couldn't leave her," she said. After Flora received a veterinary exam, visited the groomer, and started to put on weight, things began to change.

"At first, she lay on my lap or on the windowsill in the sun near my desk," Elizabeth said. "However, as she began to feel better, she demanded attention. First, she would come and rub against my legs, and then she got more demanding by climbing up them, or prancing across my keyboard. It is hard to concentrate when you have claws digging into your legs. It is also impossible to work when a cat is blocking the computer screen or covering your keyboard."

Elizabeth began making time to play with Flora. She eventually built a small garden adjacent to the window and installed an enclosed outdoor playpen for her. "Flora motivated me to do something other than work. I used to enjoy gardening, and so making her a safe outdoor haven became my weekend project. Now I just open the window and she lets herself in and out. It is large enough that I can go out and sit with her. Sometimes I read, occasionally we cuddle, and frequently we play."

Animals teach with humor and affection. They are frank about their needs, not only for food and water, but also for love, physical affection, and mental stimulation. Captive dolphins are notorious for making toys out of everything, and for their playful sexual overtures. They are comfortable with intimacy. Animals express themselves, and in doing so, they encourage their human companions to do the same.

In ordinary life, I've watched people learn how to open up and love unconditionally because their pets taught them through example. Animals motivate an inactive person to get involved in life. Animals can be a security, as well as a catalyst for new interactions with potential friends. For "commitment phobics," they are a first commitment. A mutt named Samantha was a good teacher for her pal Mason.

Mason was a lonely man who sequestered himself away to avoid any more hurt in his life. He had a failed marriage, had lost friendships, and felt he was an oddball within his own family. He became a recluse, building massive fences around his property to symbolically wall himself off and to physically protect him from outsiders. He puttered around his home tinkering with projects, and gardening. Occasionally he ventured out to see his family or go to church. Then Samantha adopted him and everything changed.

Samantha was a small black mutt with a perky personality. She loved to run and frolic in the fields. She also loved Mason with all her heart. Soon, despite himself, Mason began meeting other dogs and their owners. Initially he squirmed during these interactions, but eventually he began to look forward to them. Sometimes he joined these people for the remainder of their jaunts. Eventually, his newfound pals stopped by to ask whether he wanted to walk with them and their dogs, and ultimately these simple invitations grew to include barbecues and other social events.

During these excursions he met a woman and tentatively let her into his world. Although the relationship did not last, they remained friends. He said, "I chose not to open up completely because I was so scared. But that was a good step for me, and I feel like I am ready to try again. I realized that I truly don't want to be alone and would like to share my life with someone. Without Sam, I doubt this would have happened."

Animals exemplify many lessons, but one of the most important things they do is remind us how to be in the moment and get back to innocence when we are lost in the quagmire of our minds instead of our hearts.

One of my favorite spots in southern California is a seven-mile stretch of beach. The terrain changes drastically from day to day based on the tides, wind, and other events on the shoreline. It is always my goal to be present in the moment while I walk. However, as much as I try to be there and feel the texture of the sand, the warmth of the sun, or the dampness of the air, many times I get lost in thought as I amble up and down the beach.

Every time I visit the area, the dolphins appear, but on one of my trips I did not see any marine life. Only the shore birds entertained me. Like the issues I was struggling with, the shore break was violent and the waves that formed were huge. I pondered and sat on the shore for hours, seeking some solace from my surroundings. I prayed for the dolphins to come on the last day of my trip as I finished my final walk.

Suddenly a big set of waves came in. As the second large wave loomed near the shore, I saw them. Four bottlenose dolphins began surfing down the face of the wave, side by side. I could see every dorsal inch of their huge bodies as I gazed in amazement. They were suspended within the swell for a moment, then gone the next. For the next few waves they reappeared directly in front of me. Those moments are frozen in my memory; they took my breath away. Then, just as suddenly as they had arrived, the dolphins were gone.

Like my situation, the swell was a temporary tempest; the dolphins reminded me to ride it out and find a way to move through it, and with it. I could try to find some fun in the midst of the chaos, or I could just choose to deal with it in a manner that would bring me the quickest movement. We all can learn to apply examples from the animals if we pay attention.

Sometimes it is our household companions who bring us the most important examples in life. During one of my long walks on the beach, I met a couple who owned a dog named Rotti. They shared his story, which illustrates the way animals set examples of how to be courageous, accepting, and adventurous.

Rotti is a big Rottweiler who had a precarious start in life. Parvovirus is a deadly disease for many young dogs, and Rotti contracted it before he was eight weeks old. Surviving the disease was tough, and when he contracted it again, his new owners thought he would not survive. They were vigilant and worked hard to keep him hydrated and alive. But for weeks, he was a quiet and inactive pup. "We worried about taking him out anywhere. He was so small and had been through so much, but he had the will to live and pulled through. He accepted everything quietly," they said.

Eventually Rotti and his family ventured out to a dog beach, where he blossomed from a quiet pup into an adventurous adolescent. "He just loved the beach. He chased birds, ran up to meet any dog or person ambling along, and tried to start a game with everyone. If someone was playing ball, he joined in. He wrestled and romped with other dogs and instigated more than one game of chase. He was always exploring. The first time he went swimming he learned the hard way about waves, but soon he was out bodysurfing with us."

Rotti tried to join a group of dolphins, but he failed at battling the waves and settled onto the shore, barking out his frustration as the group swam by. Those dolphins are part of a resident group, and although they make time to play, they were engaged in a serious quest for food.

Dolphins hunt in many different ways. In some cases, success might be through their attunement to vibration, by encircling schools of fish, by whacking the prey with their tail flukes, or by trapping their fare in a constricted area. They use methods appropriate for the situation and the particular moment.

What they teach us is to hunt for the right approach and to be flexible about it. The circumstances might require a search for a way to communicate with a loved one, to address a difficult situation at work, or simply to seek help with the challenges we face. The dolphins teach us to learn from our past experiences and show us how to take advantage of the help and knowledge available from others. Following their example can make us successful in our pursuit of an ideal solution.

Remembering to Breathe

Seeking the best approach and being flexible in life requires mindfulness. The dolphin shows us how to go to great depths and withstand the pressure. During a dive, dolphins modify physically. Their bodies yield to the pressure around them and change in response. When they surface, they clear their lungs and breathe deeply.

We need to be mindful to withstand the pressures around us. Sometimes those pressures are our own burdens, or perhaps they might be responsibilities or stresses created by others. We have to deal with them. Like the dolphins, we mold to the situation and eventually restore ourselves to our original shape. If we are to grow spiritually, perhaps we can even rise above the situation and be sculpted into an enhanced version of our former self. Either way, the dolphin reminds us to breathe deeply. Like the dolphin we can cleanse and rejuvenate through breath.

Breath is life to the dolphin. Dolphins must come to the surface and be conscious of their breath at all times or they'd drown in their aquatic environment. So the dolphin must always be aware, even during sleep.

Many spiritual practices encourage focusing on the breath. When I was working in a prayer ministry, we always started our work by first breathing deeply and consciously. Many meditative groups focus on the breath, too. When we are stressed, how many of our friends remind us to breathe? To be conscious and to connect, we need to breathe! Our breath is not the only way we try to connect. Inspiration through art, movement, and other creative activities are other ways, too.

Different cultures have been fascinated with cetaceans, as seen in the frescoes, mosaics, building ornamentation, sculptures, and utensils of ancient times. Pre-Hellenic Cretans honored dolphins as gods, the ancient Greeks built a sanctuary in honor of a dolphin-god, and the Maori of New Zealand believe dolphins are messengers of the gods. More than one ancient myth involves humans transforming into dolphins and vice versa.

In Tuvalu, a small Polynesian island community, there is a legend about a plantation owner who married a dolphin. The story begins with the man's curiosity over who is invading his plants. During his quest to discover who is stealing the young leaves of his coconut trees, he notices that the raids take place during the full moon. Waiting in ambush as the next full moon rises, he discovers young adults taking the leaves valued for ceremonial skirts and chases the young men and women to the beach. As he grabs one of the young maidens, the rest jump into the sea and transform into dolphins while plunging through the waves.

He returns to the village with the maiden and marries her. Over time, they have two children. Heartsick at being trapped on the land for so long, she asks if she can return to her family in the sea. After bidding farewell to her human family, she swims off to join her dolphin clan waiting for her in the distance. The offspring of the man and the dolphin are strong and wise. Through the teachings of their mother, they become the best fishermen, and it is here the legend ends.

The idea of transmutation, or taking on the shape of an animal, is a common theme in the folklore of many nations. Many native cultures feature the idea of people becoming one with an animal and taking on the traits or spirit of the creature. Many traditions use totems, masks, or costumes to facilitate that connection.

Shamans, priestesses, priests, and other tribal advisors are traditionally the guardians of sacred knowledge. They hold the wisdom concerning the rituals that could bestow specific powers or rekindle particular energies needed by the community or by an individual. These ceremonies are important models of how to connect humans to the natural rhythms of life, and they include activities such as the donning of animal skins and masks as symbols of the important endowments being sought.

The Tuvaluan dolphin legend touches on the theme of shamanic shape-shifting described in other ancient myths and tales. These shape-shifting tales teach us how to control and shift our energies so we can draw upon those qualities when needed. Although some people consider these stories and practices to be primitive or silly, they are actually important lessons about how we can practice shifting our energies to meet the daily challenges of life.

When overwhelmed, we need to shift our energy so we can become empowered. When sluggish, we search for a source to energize us. When we are open enough to recognize ancient wisdom in symbolic content, then we can move forward to take advantage of those secrets.

Many animal behaviors serve to remind us to reconnect with the natural world. We have lost many connections to nature, and our souls cry out. These separations include distance from the natural elements and the environment, from our once-held reverence for life, and from an intimate connection to our own selves and from the divine union we seek. With the help of the animals and their lessons, we can move from fear into trust, from anger into love, and from separation into union.

My path has taken me into close proximity with creatures of all environments, and I have forged relationships with a multitude of animals. Each animal has proved to be a teacher, and each situation has been a learning experience. When I was wrapped up in a sense of invincibility, a tiger taught me that I was but a mere rag doll if he wanted me to be. A bear showed me that power could be displayed with restraint, and a vulture taught me that appearances mask loving hearts and unique beings.

You have glimpsed into the lives and habits of some amazing creatures in this book, but to really accomplish growth and obtain a visceral knowledge, you need to learn how to develop your own connections with animals. In the next chapter, you will learn how to empower your life through the animals around you.

8

Wisdom of the Owl

My meeting with a Native American couple didn't seem too unusual at the time, but I did notice the appearance of an owl, a normally nocturnal creature, who chose to fly back and forth above us throughout the duration of our conversation. Later the same evening, miles away at my home, an owl appeared and vocalized outside my window. If that wasn't enough, owls and other winged messengers visited my dreams that night. When I stumbled across an owl feather deposited on my driveway the following morning, I decided the appearances of owls in real life and in my dreams meant that I needed to pay attention.

In ancient Greece, the owl was associated with higher wisdom. There are many different folktales about this creature, and the stories about prophecy and the gifts of clairvoyance and clairaudience allude to the owl's acute vision and hearing. The owl's

In ancient Greece, the owl was associated with higher wisdom. There are many different folktales about this creature, and the stories about prophecy and the gifts of clairvoyance and clairaudience allude to the owl's acute vision and hearing. Like the owl, you must use your observational talents, remain flexible, and take what you need and discard the rest.

large eyes pick up subtle movements. Her head swivels in a large arc to allow a wider view—she is flexible. This raptor is capable of silent observation and flight, which makes her a great hunter. After consuming every part of her prey, she later discards parts with no nutritional value by regurgitating small tight bundles of bone and fur, called pellets.

To apply the spiritual lessons learned during the climb up the ladder of consciousness, you'll need to follow the example of the owl. Like the owl, you must use your observational talents, remain flexible, and take what you need and discard the rest. You can always amble up and down the ladder to review the lessons, but once you finish the climb, additional information and exercises can bring you closer to the animals in your life and reveal new skills to enhance your understanding of them. In this section, you'll find additional items to add to your tool kit.

Changing and Expanding Your Perspective

One of the biggest obstacles in human relationships with animals is ignorance about animals' intelligence, capacity to learn, and memory. Every part of the world interconnects. Recently discovered species of mammals, birds, and insects illustrate that we do not know everything about the natural world, and that we need to become caretakers of our planet or we will destroy ourselves along with it.

Animals touch a place in our souls, a deep center we also seek, sometimes consciously and sometimes not. This is the reason wild animals fascinate people. Bunnies or squirrels encountered in the woods or parks generate excitement. Without any knowledge of how to reach out to these creatures, people bribe them with food. However, this is not the connection humans seek.

If you apply the examples discussed earlier, you are already on your way to connecting with animals. Being open-minded is important. Changing your viewpoint from seeing animals as "lesser" creatures to seeing them as divine creations is another important facet. Critters reveal much more to those who treat them with respect and stop to observe and learn. Humans who make the effort to change their animal perspectives find their relationships with other living things are enhanced. These people experience new types of interactions.

Unfortunately, not everyone strides down new paths. There are still some animal training techniques that exhibit a lack of understanding. It is not necessary to force an animal into doing something, nor is it necessary to always give them treats. Many owners never realize why an animal misbehaves or how to solve the problem, and occasionally the relationship between an animal and an owner is damaged.

Breaking Convention to Create New Traditions

My pal John participated in a scent hurdle team for several years. Scent hurdling is an event where animals compete through jumps and obstacles to locate an item containing the owner's scent and retrieve it before their competitors do. One of John's pups was doing very well. Because she was a very sensitive dog, I suggested John avoid ever outfitting her with a choke or slip collar. Eventually he used those types of collars due to peer pressure and "rules." As soon as his dog experienced negativity and harshness, she began a downward spiral in her perfect performances; it was no longer a fun event.

John succumbed to the pressure of sticking to conventions and took the advice of well-meaning people with limited experience. The advice was harmful, but the good news was that we turned John's dog around by exerting a concentrated effort and by switching to a more humane training device.

Pet owners have a pretty good idea of what motivates their animals. Although some opinions are inaccurate, many hunches are right on the mark. People with animals need to know they can vary from the norm; many don't seek opinions beyond the advice of their friends or traditional training practices.

One of my group training classes contained a very happy golden retriever. He did very well in school; however, his leash manners distressed his owner. I felt he was doing great, but the owner did not. She approached me and explained her concerns.

"Buster always has his lead in his mouth. I cannot get him to leave it alone."

"Oh," I replied. "Are you planning on showing him competitively?"

"No."

"Is he damaging the leash?"

"Well, no."

"Do you have a problem with him carrying the leash? It appears that he is happy helping you hold the leash and walking you."

"No, I don't have a problem with that. But he isn't supposed to do that, is he?"

At that point, I understood her concern and explained that the goal of the class was to produce well-mannered happy dogs and delighted owners. Unlike competitive obedience, if she was comfortable, it was okay to let him continue to hold the lead. If not, we could change his actions. Buster was so content and happy that I thought it best to allow it. She enjoyed the cute behavior and the "permission" to allow it relieved her worries. The dog's behavior did not harm anyone, and because Buster was not a show dog it really didn't matter. It is okay to develop unique patterns of relationships with animals if it doesn't hurt anyone. It is also okay to go against the traditional rules of "how it is supposed to be."

Deeper Understanding through Awareness

Humans relate to the world through different personality styles. One of the more enduring theories of personality came from Galen, a Greek physician. He grouped personality traits by body fluids: sanguine (blood), choleric (yellow bile), phlegmatic (phlegm), and melancholic (black bile). Although this theory might sound a bit archaic, it influenced modern theorists.

For instance, Alfred Adler, a physician turned psychiatrist, related these types to his four personality categories. Even today, management and behavior professionals categorize the same personalities or social styles by other names. What is interesting is that I see the same four general categories exhibited in animals as well.

Each animal has specific personality traits, much like humans. These traits vary between individuals and from one species (or breed) to the next. I'd like to say I discovered this, but Ivan Pavlov (famous for his work with classical conditioning, which caused dogs to salivate when they heard a bell) used Galen's theory to describe dog personalities when he presented his work on conditioned reflexes back in 1927. Before I read his article, I worked with my own category names, and so I'd like to share them with you here. These categories apply to all animals. Each individual creature can also exhibit the traits of more than one category.

Animal Social Styles

My work with animal social styles began in 1990. Because the knowledge of human social styles assisted me in my work with pet owners and in my management roles, I assumed that identifying the same trends in animals would increase the likelihood of successful training of animals of all types. These categories are those that I named for ease of identification. Just as with humans, all animals have shades of the different categories.

Hypersensitive

Once alarmed, hypersensitive, or fear-reactive, animals cease to respond normally. These animals depended on another animal or human for guidance. Slow learners, they work best with calm, clear directives and slow, deliberate steps. Harshness or excessive reassurance does not work, because they shut down and become unable to perform; in worse cases, they panic. These critters do better in unhurried, predictable routines and with gentle training programs.

Physical traits of these animals include longer features and narrower builds. Fear-aggressive dogs, animals who retreat or hide from new people or experiences, or creatures who lash out when cornered or trapped, compose this group. They are slow or hesitant, seek to please, and are extremely devoted.

Determined

Bright, determined creatures constantly push to see what they can get away with. Quick to learn, their goal is to achieve the dominant role within the home or animal group. They exhibit aggressive movements or assertive performances, but with proper guidance become great companions or working animals. If not directed, they are a handful. These animals do better with variety and unpredictable training sessions. If given the opportunity, they often "train the trainer" or perform the bare minimum. Consistency and persistency is critical for success with these critters.

The physical characteristics in this category consist of taut body compositions and strong muscular builds. Offensively aggressive, these household animals boss their humans around. Moderate to extreme behaviors include nudging to play, rushing through doors first, demanding food, body slamming, and bumping.

Placid

Secure creatures, placid animals are always ready and willing—especially with a motivational push. These animals seldom attend training class, because they cooperate and cause little trouble. When describing these animals, people say, "My pet is an angel, we never have any trouble." In diverse collections of exotic animals, they are confident or more experienced critters. They never seem to get out of hand.

Instead of tense musculature, the physical qualities of these animals include a healthy glow and fuller features. Communication channels with these animals are good. With training, many out-of-control animals, along with their owners, mold to fit into this category.

Hyper-responsive

Swift, responsive animals are sensitive, want to please, and can learn many behaviors quickly. They work and perform well, and subtle actions trigger their behavior. Human eye contact, posture, or verbal attention (good or bad) can actually reinforce hyper-responsive behavior.

The physical tendencies of these creatures include delicate features and smaller dimensions. Fast to learn and fast to respond, these animals perform intricate tasks and behaviors. Rapt attention from humans is necessary, because these animals anticipate requests and respond accordingly.

Animal Etiquette 101

As you begin to see animal traits more clearly, you'll need time to learn more about animal etiquette. Social etiquette develops good, well-rounded, and trusting relationships with animals. Why would an animal want to deal with a stranger forcing his way into interactions? The truth is, they don't! Animals graciously tolerate many human blunders.

Humans who dislike animals always seem to get the most attention from them. Do you ever wonder why? Those people do not force animals into interactions or contact. So, animals approach them to instigate a relationship. These disinterested humans accidentally follow proper animal etiquette for cross-species (human-to-animal) interactions.

Watching and Listening

When most people talk, they cease to observe or listen to the finer details. Animals communicate differently than we do. They use subtle forms of communication, such as body language, posturing, positioning, and movement. If other animals follow the proper rules, everything is fine; if the rules are violated, there is trouble. Most animals use verbal or postural signals to warn others when the line has been crossed.

Animals have greeting rituals. Dogs greet each other, sniff nose to tail, then switch the position. This is the dog "handshake" greeting. Good manners result in companionship, exploration, play activities, or parting harmoniously. Sometimes humans mess it up by interacting with the dogs during the ritual, pulling tightly on the leash or not respecting, or noticing, any warning signs.

Each species has different rules. Let's look at primates; it is important etiquette not to stare directly into the eyes of another. That action is rude, or threatening, and violators are punished. One toothy grimace indicates fear, while another toothy grin is a direct threat. Also, direct approaches are discouraged. Knowing the nuances of these behaviors is important.

During my affiliation with one zoo, the keepers entered an enclosure housing a group of primates. These notorious monkeys tortured handlers by grabbing their hair, clothing, or tools. After working with a crew in the primate enclosure, I received an unexpected compliment. For the first time, the primates had not tortured the keepers.

By using safety measures, such as flight distance, a unified physical presence, and strategic eye contact, the animals respected our sphere and maintained their own without incident. My commonsense approach simply used what I knew about primate behavior to keep the critters at a distance. The keepers worked together instead of isolated throughout the exhibit, and I simply controlled the animals using subtle signals, movement, and spatial distance to keep the animals away from the workers. The lesson on animal etiquette rules immediately rewarded the humans!

Many people encounter problems with their birds. Birds, especially parrots and cockatoos, have specialized needs. Although most birds live in a cage, the luckier ones also have access to playpens, travel, and a variety of social interactions. Some people begin to encounter problems when their feathered friends hit sexual maturity. The animal sex drive is very strong and is the reason many birds bond with one owner and try to attack the other. Socialized birds exhibit fewer problems, but difficulties do arise, especially within the bird's territory or turf. In some households, the bird ends up in control. Bad behaviors, such as screaming, territoriality, and sometimes biting, eventually prompt owners to isolate the bird in a cage.

An owner-controlled environment or a balanced atmosphere is harmonious. When many species live together in the home it is best to develop rules early on and to stick with them. Cute baby behaviors often become nightmares later. If you let a baby bird bite when he's young, or chase other animals in the home, he'll only get worse as he matures.

Birds brought home as babies need socializing. This makes them balanced and secure. Grabbing with the beak is different from biting, and the distinction is important because some baby birds are clumsy. Proper toys and guidance teach gentleness. To avoid future problems it is important to be aware of bird behavior.

Cages housing birds at eye level or higher can contribute to misbehavior. Birds can become territorial of their cages, and if they are perched above the owner, the risk of dominance or aggressive behavior increases. High cages and playpens were once thought to provide security; however, relationship problems with these winged warriors can escalate from too many shoulder rides or high perches.

Humans exhibit a similar behavior. If you have witnessed two men yelling at each other, they attempt to get right up in each other's face, puff out their chests, and rise up on their toes. This is similar to the psychological strategy used by kings who sat on high thrones and built high castles or towers on elevated land.

Building trust and not forcing an animal are the best approaches to establishing a good relationship. Being aware of the little things makes a big difference, too. To become aware of the social etiquette of animals and build better relationships, read about their natural behavior. More important, take the time to develop understanding. Watch the animal and pay attention. Also, take the time to watch experts with a special knack. How do those people act and react around animals? What are their mannerisms? How would you describe their relationships with animals? Simply watching reveals valuable information.

How do you find an expert? You can watch professional animal trainers at local zoological parks and oceanariums and attend animal training demonstrations put on by organizations that use the latest techniques and educate the public about them. Professional animal behavior organizations have referrals to qualified professionals, and my arkanimals.com website lists referrals to qualified experts as well as informative books and tapes.

Paying Attention to Animals

If a person takes time to learn about the needs and desires of an individual animal, then communication channels open. Most behavior problems I see in pets stem from misunderstandings and miscommunication between the owners and their animals. Some animals choose people, and in other situations people choose animals, but either way it is an opportunity to learn and grow with each other.

Mahatma Gandhi said the language of nature is simple and direct. How is it that we miss those messages? Learning the language of nature is a step toward understanding. Animals communicate, and watching them is an important activity. Simple observation teaches you a new language.

The basics are the same between the different species. Some of the clues differ because of physical structure, but not by very much. Watch an animal's eyes, ears (if it has external ears), tail (or rump), posture, body tension, nostrils, mouth, and fur or hair (feathers or scales). These give subtle but clear clues as to what is transpiring.

Next, observe how the animal acts or reacts when he or she greets people. Where are the ears positioned? Is the mouth open or closed? Is there physical contact? Is there vocalization? Where is the tail? How is it moving? Is it fast or slow? Relaxed or stiff? Is there trembling in anticipation or excitement? Is the posture lowered or normal? Is there jumping?

A dog signaling happy anticipation has an open mouth, ears slightly back, and a furiously wagging tail. Sometimes the dog bows, runs, jumps, or leans against the person he is greeting. Some dogs bring the person a toy. Everything about the interaction usually telegraphs happiness.

Cats vary in their responses. Some get up to greet a person, while others wait for the visitor to come to them. There are silent, composed felines, and cats who enthusiastically dash forward to rub against legs. Some purr and some do not. Others quiver with excitement. All these signs reveal the individuality of the animal.

How does a pet react when her person leaves? Is there a difference when company arrives? Is it a different scenario with males or females, kids or adults? How does the pet act after she is scolded? What does the pet do before, during, and after meals? During playtime? Does the animal show signs of dreaming while she sleeps?

Some animals hate to be left alone. Others take no notice. Some engage in stress-related behavior such as chewing or self-mutilation when separated from their people. Many cats like to observe and do not like to interact. Each is an individual and needs to be understood as such.

Looking at an animal's different body parts is a good way to gather clues as to what he is feeling. Body tone, normal reactions, and patterns communicate what the animal is experiencing. Their bodies play a much bigger role in communicating than most of ours do.

Check out an animal's ears. Are they forward, relaxed, tense, or alert? Pinned back against the head? What is the normal position for them? Is one forward and the other sideways? How about the eyes? Are they open, half closed, relaxed, glaring, or narrow slits? Are the pupils dilated or pinpoints? What about posturing? Is the animal on his toes? Is the body posture relaxed or tense? Raised or lower than normal?

Then look at even more unusual clues. Many people miss the hair and whisker positions. Is the body fur flat or raised? Is the raised hair the same all over or just on certain parts of the body, such as the back or tail? And the whiskers! Where are they? Are they flat against the face, sticking out in front, or out to the side? Are they relaxed or tense? Is the mouth relaxed, puckered, or tense? Open or closed? Is the animal panting or breathing differently?

Make mental notes or keep a list to pick up some new clues about pets. Observing pet shows and classes provides a great training ground. Look for the fun events. When you attend beginning dog training classes, note whether the dogs like learning or not. Many do not like school and so display behavior signals that contrast with the excitement other canine students show. See whether you can determine the reasons why.

Birds and reptiles give clues, too. There is a difference in posture and body tension in a snake who is hungry and one who is simply nasty. Also, how birds fluff their feathers can mean different things. Watch to learn. What does your intuition say? Write it down in a special notebook.

Test yourself with a couple of dog examples, because everyone seems to encounter the following situations at some time or another. A dog approaches and wags his tail. He is unfamiliar. A closer look reveals the tail wag is level with his back and sometimes a bit lower; it is also relaxed. The dog's mouth is open to pant; the ears are up but not too far forward. What does this picture convey?

Another canine approaches. Her tail is held up high over her back and it is moving in a back-and-forth motion, with short, stiff wags. Her mouth is closed but looks strained and puffy, her body appears tense, and she is up on her toes. The ears are forward. What is your impression now?

Finally, you encounter another dog. This one holds his head low; his jaws are closed and his teeth are exposed; his tail is wagging but is tucked between his legs. Hair is up on parts of his back. What do you think now?

Each animal paints a different picture. The first is curious. The second is aggressive, while the third shows fear-aggression or submissiveness. In any case, it is better to avoid contact if you are unsure of an animal's intent.

Good teachers help their students solve their own problems and answer their own questions. By searching for the answer, students often come up with solutions and learn very valuable skills in the process. It does not matter whether the teacher is an animal training instructor, a spiritual leader, or a mentor at work—the important process is tapping into your own talent and connecting with your higher power.

Understanding animal communication begins through the observation of physical clues. Recognizing animal signals enables humans to handle situations *before* anything happens. Once understanding is accomplished, it is easier to move forward into other, more unusual techniques.

Sometimes You Get It, Sometimes You Don't

My colleague Jack got annoyed with me for talking to my dog. The last time we visited, he said, "You are always talking to your dog and I never hear him answer you. Do you ever get an answer?" I laughed because I *always* receive an answer. Sometimes it is a unique response; sometimes it is a polite wag that does not pull his attention away from what he is doing. If the answer is "no," his response is subtle. If it is "yes," there is more reaction or physical feedback. Jack often misses the response because it is so subtle; therefore, he does not see it or understand it. His relationship with his dogs is vastly different. With one exception, his animals live outside. My dog lives with me and sleeps on his own bed in my room. He feels like he is my son and close companion, and our relationship is complex.

Occasionally, other people's animals come up and let me know what they want. They know I pay attention and understand. Sometimes the request is for water, treats, or attention, or to be let out. They always distinguish what they want; sometimes I know exactly what the request is, while other times I guess.

Notice how some people create chaos with pets, while other people seem to calm them. Animals sense this and fall into the routine to get what they want. When you pay attention to animals, sometimes you get their messages and sometimes you don't, but your relationship will definitely change.

After mastering the art of learning the nonverbal animal signals, the next step is to notice what things pop into your mind. Sometimes they are impressions, sometimes they are ideas, and sometimes they are pictures. Pay attention to how these things come during quiet times.

Being Open and Receptive to Other Types of Information

Do your hunches come true? Hunches are examples of intuition, instincts, or telepathy. When busy, we tend to ignore them. We get occupied with other projects and forget about them, or we consider them unimportant.

As a whole, intuition is dismissed as a valuable tool in our culture. I've met many people who use concrete facts as the basis for action. Forms, policies, and procedures can be limiting. There are other pathways to get from point A to point B. Gut feelings are usually right on the mark. For instance, just before a major earthquake hit the area I lived in, I sensed something big was going to happen. All the animals, pets and wild creatures, started acting strangely twenty-four hours before the quake. Did you ever ignore a feeling and later wish you hadn't? Most people with these types of experiences invalidate them or let other people talk them out of "listening."

My gut feelings and intuitive alerts regarding animals keep me safe. After more than twenty-five years of work with animals, I have not been seriously hurt by any of them. I have gone to work with other trainers who ignored the warning signs animals give out—and with horrible consequences. Champ's story in chapter 4 is just one illustration.

As with meditative prayer, or sitting in silence, it is important to learn to quiet the mind so you can become open to hunches and intuitive connections. When quiet, you become more receptive, and if you remain open, impressions or gentle thoughts cross your mind easily. You might find yourself surprised, because impressions or pictures come when least expected. Keep a little notepad and write down your impressions. You'll see how quickly they escalate. Paying attention and validating your experiences cause them to increase.

Next, start focusing specifically on animals. Trust your impressions and keep your mind from wandering or chattering. Perhaps you may "feel" your animal wants to have a snack or go outside. Whatever impression you receive, act on it. Start with small, simple things, such as what the animal wants. Is it food, water, playtime, attention, or something else? Do you receive mental pictures or impressions? Just observe, and don't judge.

Without interpreting, wait for more experiences. Start with animals you know. Most intuitive experiences come from the people and animals closest to you. When you get more experienced and secure, you might approach other animals in the same way.

When I first began using this technique with strange animals, I attempted to connect with a zoo tiger. The tiger became annoyed, looked at me with his ears half back and a scowl on his face, and moved away from me to the back of the exhibit! Others welcomed the attempt and greeted me in return. Another tiger ventured over to where I stood, rubbed the bars to solicit contact, and softly vocalized.

Each animal and species has individual likes and dislikes. The differences make some amiable and others resentful of an intrusion. My impression is that the more positive associations animals have with humans and the more exposure or socialization they are given to different events, people, and interactions, the more they become willing to interact. Do not impose or force animals into anything. Good etiquette means you ask for permission to interact with any animal; sometimes you need to ask a human, but you should also ask the animal or let him make the first move.

Moving Animals from Group Consciousness to Individuality

Animals do have awareness. Some dwell in a group mentality while others have a greater sense of individuality. People ask about the "group consciousness" of animals. This refers to animals reacting through instincts more than anything else. Animals living in the wild exhibit this tendency, as do prey species (those hunted by predatory animals) and many creatures living in group situations where they are reliant on one leader for guidance.

Humans tend to look for leadership as well. Sometimes the group behavior is to follow the leader, such as in cultic activities, or to follow the crowd, as in mob mentality. We need to cling to the rungs of the spiritual ladder and pull ourselves up, rather than putting someone else up on a pedestal. Our lesson is not to follow charismatic teachers unthinkingly; instead, we are to select and learn through their guidance and examples. Good leaders generate capable and compassionate people.

Animals also blossom and become complex beings under good leadership. I suspect this is due to stimulation and education. Living with humans in a stimulating environment, whether as a domestic companion or as a captive creature, catapults development forward in ways other animals don't experience.

For instance, a number of years ago I assisted a young ewe (a female sheep) named Jill. Jill was a former 4-H project, and the family now wanted to make her an integral part of their home. The parents wanted to give their daughter a challenging task and keep the ewe occupied. It is possible to train almost any creature, and so we began with the first step: getting the animal's interest and attention. I proceeded to call the ewe's name and each time I called, Jill received a treat at the same time. We repeated this process.

Next, I slowly withdrew and required Jill to move toward me to receive the reward. Eventually she understood the concept. Instead of merely standing there when I said her name, she responded. The owner exclaimed, "The lightbulb just went on! I saw it!" Many people do not see the shift occur, but she observed the animal moving into another level of response and understanding. Once accomplished, the animal made a choice instead of just reacting. The ewe had shifted into another level of awareness and became individualized. From that point forward, she recognized her given name and the consequences of correct responses. No longer "just" a member of the flock, she was primed for learning.

Caretakers who respect their charges and shower them with affection and guidance help them become more social. These critters, familiar with human social rules, are much more playful.

Even captive animals exhibit likes and dislikes. Sometimes they engage in "joke" behaviors to make a point. One Siberian tiger I worked with merely tolerated me. He had eyes only for the woman who raised him and consequently "put up" with other humans. Raja was creative in his attempts to amuse himself. I used caution around him and strived to remain aware of his activities, because if given the opportunity he would try to maim or kill. Once, while I was totally focused on a project involving another animal, I drifted within Raja's range. When I stood up and stepped back, my peripheral vision caught movement.

Raja stretched and waved his paw in the air about three feet from me in an attempt to grab me. As I gasped and moved back, he pulled his paw in, got a satisfied "twinkle" in his eye, and began to bounce around his enclosure. He had finally caught me by surprise and it made his day. He ran and leapt and grabbed his toy. As he bit down into his truck tire, he shook it violently. Raja stared at me intently during the process, just to show me what he intended if I was within reach! We had a good mutual understanding. There was no mistake in his delight and in his malice.

Acknowledging Your Hunches, Taking Action, and Trying New Techniques

We have a responsibility to be caretakers of the animals and the earth. Until we understand the living creatures we love, dominate, destroy, control, and fear, we cannot possibly operate from a solid base of compassion and understanding. We need to take our lessons further into action.

Most people dismiss what they feel or suspect, especially if others tell them it is nonsense. Ignore them. Have fun and acknowledge the hunches and experiences coming your way. Things will get easier as you do. As your process becomes second nature, animals will come to "tell" you things. Remember to pay attention. Traditionally, animals strive for attention. Because most people ignore well-behaved animals, many animals learn to be obnoxious in order to obtain attention!

On a visit with new clients, I ventured into their yard to observe their dogs and their interactions. The owners asked me why one of the dogs jumped up all the time and also backed up against human legs.

As I observed the tiny Shetland sheepdog, he jumped for attention. Also a submissive animal, he backed up onto people's legs to get noticed. During my assessment, he started jumping on me. Instead of reinforcing the behavior by petting him, I said, "No. What should you do instead?" He stopped and looked at me intently. With his ears forward, he linked his eyes with mine and backed away. I said, "That's right, and what else?" Then I visualized what I wanted.

As we gazed at each other, I pictured him sitting in front of me. I did not say a word. Everyone else was transfixed. He looked at me and firmly planted his rear on the ground in a sit. I said, "Good for you. That's right!" Then I immediately petted and praised him. The owners shook their heads in disbelief.

Another step toward better communication with animals involves picturing what you want. Mental picturing is used in many management and goal-setting sessions, but it is much like daydreaming. Try it. Think of floating in a nice pool on a very hot day. Picture the blueness of the sky and feel the rhythm of the water. As the sun beats down, feel the warmth in contrast to the comfort of floating in the pool. Can you picture it? How about a red apple? Think about a delicious, red, shiny apple. It is perfect, with a short stem shooting out from the top. It also tapers from a wide point at the stem area down to the base. The color is ruby red, deep, crisp, and brilliant.

Visualization is picturing your pet doing the proper behavior. You might need to do some animal training, too, but many people who call their animal to "come" experience problems because they visualize the pet running away, or avoiding them, instead of coming. The pet gets the picture, thinks it is a good game, and receives accidental reinforcement through the drama of pursuit.

One of my clients owns a big white dog who loved to run away and bark when asked to come in. Living on a rural property, the frustrated owner spent hours trying to capture her dog. Our first efforts involved narrowing the escape area and teaching him to come. Because the owner was not consistent with him, he was not consistent with her. Sometimes she gave up right away and left him out, while at other times she persisted. The dog learned to get his way by not relenting.

However, he never gave me trouble. I visualized and expected the correct behavior and if he did not cooperate, he knew I would persevere. To this day, he immediately comes to me instead of making me pursue him.

Fortunately, more and more people are considering alternative ways to deal with animals. Although you might not be aware of how much you intuit, others around you may reveal information verifying your success. This happens to me often, but one situation in particular makes me smile.

Each morning, as I made the rounds to check on the animals at a local humane society, I greeted all the dogs and the cats housed there. One particular animal was named Satin. No matter how hard I tried to call him by his name, I always ended up calling him Satan. It was bizarre. I checked his name tag daily, but still struggled to call him by the right name. Despite my best efforts, this did not help me. One day the kennel manager overheard me. Wanda laughed. When I looked up, she commented, "You are calling him by his original name." Wanda told me his story.

When Satan arrived, he behaved like a monster. As time passed and he received love and attention, he changed into a very loving and outgoing animal. The staff decided to change his name and his image.

Wanda felt I had picked up on the information without knowing the full story.

Another memorable experience occurred during a group dog training class. One dog student did not understand what his owner wanted. At the time, we were teaching a simple "sit." After a few attempts by the owner, I assisted the duo without any explanation.

After I visualized what I wanted the dog to do, he looked closely at me and slowly sat. His success was rewarded with treats and praise from the entire group. The wheels began to turn in his mind and he showed excitement. After that, learning became easier for him. He paid attention and took risks by responding. Although unsure in the beginning, he learned to think and to look for guidance.

After class, the other dog owners came up to me to ask whether I had visualized what I wanted the dog to do. They intuitively felt and physically saw another type of communication, witnessed the result, and were excited to learn about the process.

Deep communication requires accountability and attentiveness to the animal. The simplest way to test the effectiveness of visualization is by working with your animal. Picture your pet fetching her favorite toy or receiving a treat and wait for the response.

My dog does not normally work for treats, so he gets excited when I ask him to do behaviors in exchange for tidbits. Because he knows both verbal and signal commands, I use a goody to encourage him to "picture" what I want. I hold a morsel and ask him, "What are you supposed to do?" and then I visualize the behavior. If he does the right behavior, he gets the treat. If not, we begin again, or we quit and try later. It is easy to see whether an animal is tapping into the pictures by the way he looks at you. In most cases, the animal focuses intently on your face, ears attentive and physically quiet.

Another method I use is "dialoguing." This is where I talk to an animal and verbalize what he shares. This occurs when I am involved in animal interactions and not fully aware of the process. Sometimes the responses surprise me.

My coworkers chuckled and shook their heads when I chattered with the elephants. One day, when the elephants were especially feisty, we readied the performers for the next show. When one elephant, Deirdre, showed up at the show arena gates, I believed she wanted to perform, but it was too late. I explained this to her and promised to work her in the arena after the presentation if she returned later. I then muttered something as though she had responded. My fellow trainers teased me no end.

Because the performance marked the end of our hectic mornings, many of the elephants came down to the arena after the show for individual attention. When my pachyderm pal came back at the end of that particular event, she didn't just want attention, she wanted admittance into the show area. I made a deal with Deirdre and had no doubt that she understood and responded to my promise. The guys rolled their eyes, but Deirdre and I enjoyed a great training session.

When you are in the beginning stages of exploring and learning new techniques, do not rely on food or tricks, because they defeat the purpose. Work at building a better relationship and mutual interactions. Come up with your own ideas on how to be more receptive and innovative. As you work on fine-tuning your animal skills, don't forget about sharpening your efforts with humans.

Using Your Imagination and Creativity

Another step in developing animal communication skills is to start using your imagination. We tend to think about things from a human perspective. Learning to relate from an animal's perspective can open up new doors to understanding and compassion. Think for a moment about how animals see things. At what level do they look at things? Do they see colors? Shadows? Views of people from the ground can make them look like giants. Get down on ground level and look up at someone. Is it disconcerting? What could be perceived as harmful or dangerous? How does natural instinct affect the animal? Play with this idea.

One of the first tigers I trained transferred her natural instinct to avoid humans into a fear of inanimate objects. It surprised me when, during our walks, she suddenly tensed and locked her gaze onto something. One time we walked by the elephant barn, and she became fearful. I stopped, got down on her level, and watched with her. As I talked to her, I encouraged her to approach the barn. I walked toward the barn and to the end of her lead (they are called "cat chains" and are a *big* animal version of a leash), stopped, and crouched down. She slowly advanced and attempted to crawl into my lap for security! Gradually we got closer and closer to the *huge* menacing building with the big black open mouth. As we entered the barn, she discovered there was no threat, and she relaxed. Fortunately, the elephants were playing outside in their pasture.

Another time, she feared the feed truck. Again, inch by inch we approached the "scary monster," until the young tiger perched confidently on the back of the truck. This type of preliminary training is important for animals. Many react fearfully to new circumstances or people if they are not socialized or desensitized to various objects. This is similar to the "monster under the bed" concern kids must overcome. It always amazes me when I look at things from the animal perspective. They are quick to react and have such different perspectives that I see life from an entirely new angle.

Animals exhibit a unique sense of humor that varies from species to species and among individuals. During my interactions with elephants, I continually delighted at their silliness. Elephants are extremely intelligent and sensitive creatures. The last herd I worked with included some of the most stable and wonderful elephants I have ever met. They were also very mischievous. During the shows I tried to teach the audience how to identify the animals as individuals and pointed out their particular characteristics.

Deirdre was impish. When excited, she would fidget with her trunk. She made up new sounds or variations on behaviors in the hopes of finagling additional rewards. Deirdre also tested us by reducing her performance to the lowest level for which she could get rewarded. She was bored with it all.

Because of the lack of constancy among the different trainers, she decided to trumpet on command, but only on the second attempt. This unacceptable response was difficult to correct because some of the trainers rewarded it. So, Deirdre and I began working on a different behavior, distinguished as "*big* trumpet." To qualify for a reward, she needed to trumpet loudly on the first attempt. If she responded correctly, she was rewarded; if she was lazy, we moved on to something else. Because Deirdre loved the challenge of meeting my criteria for the behavior, she quickly responded.

Finally, we brought the behavior into the show. Dubbed "assistant trainers," the audience knew about the challenge and was prepared to erupt in wild applause if Deirdre was successful. As they sat in quiet expectation, you could hear a pin drop. When the command was given, Deirdre took a deep breath and then trumpeted loudly. The audience went crazy; I went wild, hopping up and down telling her, "Good job, good job!" Deirdre got animated and flapped her ears and fidgeted with her trunk. The audience saw her excitement. We ended the show on that high note and invited the onlookers to come down and ask questions. Obtaining the proper response required an understanding of what motivated Deirdre as an individual. Individuals respond differently. Knowing a species or a breed is not enough—you must pay attention to details and to the individual. Each animal conveys information in a variety of ways.

For example, the owl uses the senses of hearing and sight and the cloak of silence to successfully hunt. She knows when to sit and observe, when to change perspective, and when to flap her wings or swiftly swoop toward her target. We, too, must use all our senses and be in the proper state of mind to reap the benefits of our work and allow it to become second nature—that is, effortless.

Afterword: Creatures of the Divine

Being open and receptive helps us cultivate new insights and helps us grow. The growth process requires that we continue to explore and challenge our thought processes. A book about how animals help us spiritually remains incomplete without discussing whether or not animals have souls, so I thought it fitting to end on that topic.

In all my years in the Big Bear Valley, I spent a lot of time at one of my favorite spots, an area overlooking the valley and the desert. Clyde, my loyal dog, and I spent many hours hiking through the surrounding trails, and I invested many more just sitting and contemplating life from atop a sacred site simply known as "The Eye of God." Although Clyde had no need to reflect, he loved the area, too. He'd run ahead of my truck on our way to the trailhead, and then he loped ahead of me on each footpath—catching exciting scents and following them until he was done exploring. Clyde indulged me with his presence on top of the rock site, but only for short stints. As he aged our trips became less frequent, until he could no longer manage the long jaunt at all.

Then, heartbreak struck. Clyde's looming euthanasia appointment was imminent. Nothing made the process easier. Despite my trusted intuition, I contacted an animal communicator for help. In my quest to do everything to make the transition as easy as possible, I learned that Clyde wanted two things—three days to prepare, and one last trip to "The Eye of God."

So there I was, lugging Clyde, poised regally inside an all-terrain red wagon, up to the sacred site overlooking the entire valley. I don't know how long Clyde and I sat up there, but the picture of him in the wagon is indelibly etched in my mind.

Losing a loved one is probably the most difficult thing we can experience. Nothing can fill the void left by the loss of his or her unique spirit, and nothing can describe the agony of the grief process. Although I've experienced many losses, none is so fresh or so deep as that of my Clyde. I never expected a dog to become my guardian, my companion, my playmate, my dog-training assistant, or my surrogate son, but Clyde was all those things. Clyde taught me important rules:

Love deeply, because it is all that matters.
Greet those you love with enthusiasm.
Make time for loved ones before anything else.
Don't forget to love yourself.
Forgive quickly and move on.
Be loyal to family and friends.
See the good in everyone and enjoy the interactions you have.
Make others smile.
Play every day.
Go for walks.
Take naps.
Enjoy your meals.
Pay attention to the moment.
Do your best no matter what.
Make mistakes and try again, because that is how you learn.
Be the first to make up.

In those last days, I reflected on the lessons Clyde had shared and decided he was indeed a great teacher. I spent every minute with Clyde, and I felt the exact moment the life force left his body—for I was holding him. Clyde was a divine creation. All animals are.

The love of God is for all creatures. However, this does not prevent people from enslaving humans or regarding others as second-class beings. Not too long ago, the dispute over souls was not about animals, but about whether or not certain ethnic groups and women had eternal souls.

It is fitting that I am writing this piece exactly a year after Clyde left this physical plane. The word "animal" is derived from the Latin word *anima,* which translates as soul. Do I believe animals have souls? Yes, I do. And 86 percent of readers surveyed by Belief.net, a multifaith Internet community dedicated to spiritual and religious topics, believe it, too.

The theories about animals lacking souls or spirit are just that— theories. Both philosophers and theologians have spouted their opinions over the centuries. In the ancient world, Aristotle questioned whether souls were a plurality or simply the plurality of the parts of one soul. Plato claimed the souls of all living creatures were part of the universal soul of the world. Disciples of Socrates maintained that a human possessed a rational soul above the animal, and Saint Augustine was interested in animals only in relation to their physical or spiritual benefit to humans.

Negative views on animal souls appear rooted in two philosophers' opinions. Thomas Aquinas, a thirteenth-century Italian philosopher and theologian, discussed animal and human souls in the *Summa Theologica.* In the seventeenth century, the French philosopher René Descartes insisted animals were not capable of thinking, were not intelligent, did not have language, were mere biological machines, and did not experience pleasure or pain. Contemporary studies of animal physiology, intelligence, and language capabilities have proved otherwise.

English philosopher Jeremy Bentham, writing in the early 1800s, did not think it appropriate to ask whether animals reasoned or talked; rather, he asked, "Can they suffer?" Charles Darwin, in *The Expression of the Emotions in Man and Animals*, proposed that the difference between the inner lives of humans and animals is one of degree, not of kind.

Various translations of Hebrew Scripture exist, but in the Book of Genesis, translation errors seem to muddle the question. *The Immortality of Animals*, written in 1903 by Elijah D. Buckner, discusses how the phrase *nephesh chayah* literally translates as "living soul," but Genesis passages using the same phrase have been translated differently when referring to humans and animals. References to humans were translated as "living soul," while animal references were translated as "living creature." In January 1990, Pope John Paul II said, "Also the animals possess a soul and men must love and feel solidarity with smaller brethren." He referred to the same passages in Genesis.

According to Buckner's book, religions of Egypt and Phoenicia, Islam, Brahmanism (Hinduism), Zoroastrianism, Buddhism, Greek and Norse religions, Confucianism, and "primitive religions" of the world directly or indirectly advocate the immortality of animals.

Other books, such as *Do Dogs Go to Heaven?* by M. Jean Holmes, *The Soul of Your Pet* by Scott S. Smith, and *Animal Gospel* by Andrew Linzey, explore additional religious and philosophical opinions on the topic. *The Soul of Your Pet* states that Christian Scientists and the Church of Jesus Christ of Latter-day Saints both have writings that suggest the individual identity of animals and living souls, but that Jehovah's Witnesses do not, and Seventh-day Adventists believe there is no biblical basis for any doctrine on the subject. In addition, the Japanese religion of Shinto acknowledges that all things contain *kami*, or spirit, and Jainism, a derivative of Hinduism, regards all souls as sacred and indestructible.

In his popular book, *The Souls of Animals*, Gary Kowalski, a

Unitarian Universalist minister, states with conviction that he believes animals have souls. In his book, he discusses whether animals are aware of death, know right from wrong, experience love, and are conscious of themselves. These are questions I take for granted because my experiences answer those questions affirmatively. I've watched animals blossom and grow in their awareness and become individual personalities. The little ewe, Jill, was just one example.

When it comes to discussing eternal life, *The Soul of Your Pet* shares anecdotes about animals in the afterlife through human witnesses. Visions, astral travel, out-of-body experiences, and animal communication stories form part of his book. Smith discovered that the lack of reports of animals in the hereafter were due to the fact that researchers failed to ask about them. Psychiatrist Dr. Milton Hadley, a former Cambridge University associate, documented hundreds of pet encounters, and parapsychologist D. Scott Rugo shared two animal accounts in Smith's work.

My belief in the Divine comforts me and gives me peace. When Clyde left his body, I felt his essence leave and his spiritual form run off. I hope that the life energy of animals I have known indeed dwell elsewhere. These amazing creatures were significant in my life and growth.

Saint Francis of Assisi grasped the spiritual significance of animals. As Saint Francis got closer to God, he found he was able to commune with animals. As we get closer to animals, and to God, we can find that same communion.

Since the dawn of humankind, we have desired to live in harmony with all creation, to feel a connection to animals and the Divine. Animals might just be more tangible connections, bridges to the celestial. Watch them. Learn from them, and use the lessons and exercises in this book to find your connection. This is not the end; it is the beginning of a new journey.

Best wishes on your spiritual safari.

Suggested Resources

Because this book was written from my experience, I thought it best to give you some additional resources. This list represents a selection of works I believe will be useful in helping you understand animals. I invite you to visit my website at www.arkanimals.com to peruse my latest works and other animal books and videos.

Alderton, David. *Wild Cats of the World*. New York: Sterling Publications, 1998.

Bauer, Erwin. *Bears: Behavior, Ecology, Conservation*. Stillwater, Minn.: Voyageur Press, 1998.

Bekoff, Marc. *Minding Animals*. New York: Oxford University Press, 2002.

Benyus, Janine M. *The Secret Language and Remarkable Behavior of Animals*. New York: Black Dog & Leventhal Publishers, 1998.

Bonner, Nigel. *Seals and Sea Lions of the World*. New York: Facts on File, 1994.

Brown, Gary. *Safe Travel in Bear Country*. New York: Lyons Press, 1996.

Buckner, Elijah D. *The Immortality of Animals*. Philadelphia: Jacobs, 1903.

Campbell, William. *The New Better Behavior in Dogs*. Loveland, Colo.: Alpine Publications, 1999.

Chadwick, Douglas H. *The Fate of the Elephant*. San Francisco: Sierra Club Books, 1992.

Chance, Paul. *Learning and Behavior*. 3rd ed. Pacific Grove, Calif.: Brooks/Cole Publishing, 1998.

Coren, Stanley. *The Intelligence of Dogs*. New York: Free Press, 1994.

Dodman, Nicholas. *The Cat Who Cried for Help*. New York: Bantam Doubleday Dell, 1999.

———. *The Dog Who Loved Too Much*. New York: Bantam Books, 1997.

Douglas-Hamilton, Iain, et al. *African Elephants: A Celebration of Majesty*. New York: Abbeville Press, 1998.

Fisher, Betty. *Caninestein*. New York: HarperCollins, 1997.

———. *So Your Dog's Not Lassie*. New York: HarperCollins, 1998.

Fogel, Bruce. *The Cat's Mind*. New York: Macmillan, 1995.

Fouts, Roger S. *Next of Kin*. New York: William Morrow, 1997.

Fowler, Murray. *Restraint and Handling of Wild and Domestic Animals*. Iowa City: Iowa University Press, 1995.

Fox, Michael. *Understanding Your Cat*. New York: St. Martin's Press, 1992.

Gittleman, John, ed. *Carnivore Behavior, Ecology, and Evolution*. Ithaca, N.Y.: Comstock Publishing, 1996.

Goodall, Jane. *In the Shadow of Man*. Rev. ed. Boston: Houghton Mifflin, 2000.

———. *Through a Window*. Boston: Houghton Mifflin, 1990.

Grzimeck, Bernhard, ed. *Grzimeck's Animal Life Encyclopedia*. Vols. 1–13. New York: Van Nostrand Reinhold, 1972.

Hall-Martin, Anthony, ed. *Cats of Africa*. Washington, D.C.: Smithsonian Institution Press, 1998.

Holmes, M. Jean. *Do Dogs Go to Heaven? Eternal Answers for Animal Lovers*. Tulsa, Okla.: JoiPax Publishing, 1999.

Hornocker, Maurice, ed. *Track of the Tiger*. San Francisco: Sierra Club Books, 1997.

Houpt, Katherine. *Domestic Animal Behavior for Veterinarians and Animal Scientists*. Iowa City: Iowa State University Press, 1998.

Kazdin, Alan E. *Behavior Modification in Applied Settings*. Pacific Grove, Calif.: Brooks/Cole Publishing, 1994.

Kleiman, Devra G., ed. *Wild Mammals in Captivity*. Chicago: University of Chicago Press, 1997.

Kowalski, Gary. *The Souls of Animals*. Walpole, N.H.: Stillpoint Publishing, 1991.

Lachman, Larry. *Birds off the Perch*. New York: Fireside Press, 2003.

———. *Cats on the Counter*. New York: St. Martin's Press, 2001.

———. *Dogs on the Couch*. New York: Overlook Press, 1999.

Landsberg, Gary, et al. *Handbook of Behavior Problems of the Dog and Cat*. Newton, Mass.: Butterworth-Heinemann Medical, 1997.

Linzey, Andrew. *Animal Gospel*. Louisville, Ky.: Westminster/John Knox Press, 1999.

Linzey, A., and D. Yamamoto, eds. *Animals on the Agenda*. Champaign: University of Illinois Press, 1998.

MacDonald, David, ed. *The Encyclopedia of Mammals*. New York: Facts on File, 1995.

Marlo, Shelby. *Shelby Marlo's New Art of Dog Training*. New York: Contemporary Books, 1999.

Masson, Jeffrey Moussaieff, and Susan McCarthy. *When Elephants Weep: The Emotional Lives of Animals*. New York: Delacorte, 1991.

Mazur, James E. *Learning and Behavior*. Englewood Cliffs, N.J.: Prentice Hall, 1994.

McElroy, Susan Chernak. *Animals as Teachers and Healers: True Stories and Reflections*. New York: Ballantine, 1998.

McFarland, David, ed. *The Oxford Companion to Animal Behavior*. New York: Oxford University Press, 1987.

Milani, Myrna. *Catsmart*. New York: NTC/Contemporary, 1998.

Monks of New Skete. *The Art of Raising a Puppy*. Boston: Little, Brown, 1991.

Nowak, Ronald, ed. *Walker's Mammals of the World*. Baltimore: Johns Hopkins University Press, 1999.

Payne, Katy. *Silent Thunder: In the Presence of Elephants*. New York: Simon & Schuster, 1998.

Payne, Roger. *The Whale Watchers Guide*. Chanhassen, Minn.: NorthWord Press, 1999.

Pringle, Laurence, and Cynthia Moss. *Elephant Woman: Cynthia Moss Explores the World of Elephants*. New York: Atheneum, 1997.

Pryor, Karen. *Don't Shoot the Dog!* New York: Bantam Books, 1999.

Ryan, Terry. *The Toolbox for Remodeling Your Problem Dog*. New York: Howell Book House, 1998.

Schneider, Bill. *Bear Aware: Hiking and Camping in Bear Country*. Guilford, Conn.: Falcon, 1996.

Shepherdson, David, ed. *Second Nature: Environmental Enrichment for Captive Animals*. Washington, D.C.: Smithsonian Institution Publications, 1998.

Shoshani, Jeheskel, ed. *Elephants*. New York: Simon & Schuster, 1992.

Smith, David. *Backcountry Bear Basics*. Seattle: Mountaineers Books, 1997.

Smith, Scott S. *The Soul of Your Pet*. Edmonds, Wash.: Holmes Publishing Group, 1998.

Smuts, Barbara B. *Sex and Friendship in Baboons*. Cambridge, Mass.: Harvard University Press, 1999.

Sukumar, Raman. *Elephant Days and Nights: Ten Years with the Indian Elephant*. New York: Oxford University Press, 1996.

———. *The Asian Elephant: Ecology and Management*. New York: Cambridge University Press, 1993.

Turner, Alan, et al. *The Big Cats and Their Fossil Relatives.* New York: Columbia University Press, 1997.

Volhard, Joachim. *The Canine Good Citizen.* New York: Howell Book House, 1997.

de Waal, Frans. *Chimpanzee Politics.* Baltimore: Johns Hopkins University Press, 1998.

Acknowledgments

The stories in this book come from my life and to thank everyone who has contributed is impossible. Here I have room to say that I am immensely grateful to everyone, but I can list only those who directly contributed to this book.

First, I must thank the publishing team at SkyLight Paths—you are a writer's dream. Special gratitude goes to Stuart M. Matlins, Jon M. Sweeney, Emily Wichland, Lauren Seidman, Bridgett Taylor, Drena Fagen, and Karen Levy. *Muchas gracias* to Shelly Angers for introducing me to my editor. Shelly, without you this book would not have been written. To my editor and project partner, Maura D. Shaw: I adore you. My sincere thanks for your amazing support and spirit.

My admiration and gratitude for comments and suggestions go to fellow scribes and friends: Coral Wilson, Lee Födi, Jo-ed Griffith, Rita Robinson, and Elizabeth "Libby" Grandy.

Special thanks and recognition must go to my cheerleading squad for their love, encouragement, and support: Stephanie Jefferson, Tom Averill, Angela Carolyn and Lawrence Enroth, Chris McCormick, Margaret and Reinhard Tiefenthaler, Raymond Martin, Elivia Melodey, Suzanne Szames, Madelon and Paul Hendel, Gregory Randall, Sandy

Wilson, and Natalie A. Hofmans. Love to my fairy godmother incarnate, Ahmee Burt. To Becky and Karl Francis: Thanks for your understanding and support, and the red wagon.

For the inspiration and encouragement to pursue my writing from the first time we met, I must thank Diane Grindol. To my friend and column editor, Susan Chan: I am thankful for your support and understanding. To the members of the Alliance of Writers and the Inland Empire Chapter of the California Writer's Club: I value your support and camaraderie. To Dale Anderson and the gang at the Sierra Endangered Cat Haven: Thanks for many things, including the fabulous photo opportunity with Camlo.

Finally, my heartfelt thanks to God, as spirit everywhere present, and to all the animals who taught me about what really matters.

About SKYLIGHT PATHS Publishing

SkyLight Paths Publishing is creating a place where people of different spiritual traditions come together for challenge and inspiration, a place where we can help each other understand the mystery that lies at the heart of our existence.

Through spirituality, our religious beliefs are increasingly becoming a part of our lives—rather than *apart* from our lives. While many of us may be more interested than ever in spiritual growth, we may be less firmly planted in traditional religion. Yet, we do want to deepen our relationship to the sacred, to learn from our own as well as from other faith traditions, and to practice in new ways.

SkyLight Paths sees both believers and seekers as a community that increasingly transcends traditional boundaries of religion and denomination—people wanting to learn from each other, *walking together, finding the way.*

We at SkyLight Paths take great care to produce beautiful books that present meaningful spiritual content in a form that reflects the art of making high quality books. Therefore, we want to acknowledge those who contributed to the production of this book.

PRODUCTION
Tim Holtz & Bridgett Taylor

EDITORIAL
Lauren Seidman, Maura D. Shaw & Emily Wichland

COVER DESIGN
Bridgett Taylor

TYPESETTING
Kristin Goble, PerfecType, Nashville, Tennessee

PRINTING & BINDING
Versa Press, East Peoria, Illinois

Other Interesting Books—Spirituality

Lighting the Lamp of Wisdom: *A Week Inside a Yoga Ashram*
by *John Ittner*; Foreword by *Dr. David Frawley*

This insider's guide to Hindu spiritual life takes you into a typical week of retreat inside a yoga ashram to demystify the experience and show you what to expect from your own visit. Includes a discussion of worship services, meditation and yoga classes, chanting and music, work practice, and more.

6 x 9, 192 pp, b/w photographs, Quality PB, ISBN 1-893361-52-7 **$15.95**; HC, ISBN 1-893361-37-3 **$24.95**

Waking Up: *A Week Inside a Zen Monastery*
by *Jack Maguire*; Foreword by *John Daido Loori, Roshi*

An essential guide to what it's like to spend a week inside a Zen Buddhist monastery.

6 x 9, 224 pp, b/w photographs, Quality PB, ISBN 1-893361-55-1 **$16.95**; HC, ISBN 1-893361-13-6 **$21.95**

Making a Heart for God: *A Week Inside a Catholic Monastery*
by *Dianne Aprile*; Foreword by *Brother Patrick Hart*, OCSO

This essential guide to experiencing life in a Catholic monastery takes you to the Abbey of Gethsemani—the Trappist monastery in Kentucky that was home to author Thomas Merton—to explore the details. "More balanced and informative than the popular *The Cloister Walk* by Kathleen Norris." —*Choice: Current Reviews for Academic Libraries*

6 x 9, 224 pp, b/w photographs, Quality PB, ISBN 1-893361-49-7 **$16.95**; HC, ISBN 1-893361-14-4 **$21.95**

Come and Sit: *A Week Inside Meditation Centers*
by *Marcia Z. Nelson*; Foreword by *Wayne Teasdale*

The insider's guide to meditation in a variety of different spiritual traditions. Traveling through Buddhist, Hindu, Christian, Jewish, and Sufi traditions, this essential guide takes you to different meditation centers to meet the teachers and students and learn about the practices, demystifying the meditation experience.

6 x 9, 224 pp, b/w photographs, Quality PB, ISBN 1-893361-35-7 **$16.95**

Spiritual Practice

Women Pray
Voices through the Ages, from Many Faiths, Cultures, and Traditions
Edited and with introductions by *Monica Furlong*

Many ways—new and old—to communicate with the Divine.

This beautiful gift book celebrates the rich variety of ways women around the world have called out to the Divine—with words of joy, praise, gratitude, wonder, petition, longing, and even anger—from the ancient world up to our own time. Prayers from women of nearly every religious or spiritual background give us an eloquent expression of what it means to communicate with God. 5 x 7¼, 256 pp, Deluxe HC with ribbon marker, ISBN 1-893361-25-X **$19.95**

Praying with Our Hands: *Twenty-One Practices of Embodied Prayer from the World's Spiritual Traditions*
by *Jon M. Sweeney*; Photographs by *Jennifer J. Wilson*;
Foreword by *Mother Tessa Bielecki*; Afterword by *Taitetsu Unno, Ph.D.*

A spiritual guidebook for bringing prayer into our bodies.

This inspiring book of reflections and accompanying photographs shows us twenty-one simple ways of using our hands to speak to God, to enrich our devotion and ritual. All express the various approaches of the world's religious traditions to bringing the body into worship. Spiritual traditions represented include Anglican, Sufi, Zen, Roman Catholic, Yoga, Shaker, Hindu, Jewish, Pentecostal, Eastern Orthodox, and many others.
8 x 8, 96 pp, 22 duotone photographs, Quality PB, ISBN 1-893361-16-0 **$16.95**

The Sacred Art of Listening
Forty Reflections for Cultivating a Spiritual Practice
by *Kay Lindahl*; Illustrations by *Amy Schnapper*

More than ever before, we need to embrace the skills and practice of listening. You will learn to: Speak clearly from your heart • Communicate with courage and compassion • Heighten your awareness for deep listening • Enhance your ability to listen to people with different belief systems. 8 x 8, 160 pp, Illus., Quality PB, ISBN 1-893361-44-6 **$16.95**

Labyrinths from the Outside In
Walking to Spiritual Insight—a Beginner's Guide
by *Donna Schaper* and *Carole Ann Camp*

The user-friendly, interfaith guide to making and using labyrinths— for meditation, prayer, and celebration.

Labyrinth walking is a spiritual exercise *anyone* can do. This accessible guide unlocks the mysteries of the labyrinth for all of us, providing ideas for using the labyrinth walk for prayer, meditation, and celebrations to mark the most important moments in life. Includes instructions for making a labyrinth of your own and finding one in your area.
6 x 9, 208 pp, b/w illus. and photographs, Quality PB, ISBN 1-893361-18-7 **$16.95**

SkyLight Illuminations Series
Andrew Harvey, series editor

Offers today's spiritual seeker an enjoyable entry into the great classic texts of the world's spiritual traditions. Each classic is presented in an accessible translation, with facing pages of guided commentary from experts, giving you the keys you need to understand the history, context, and meaning of the text. This series enables readers of all backgrounds to experience and understand classic spiritual texts directly, and to make them a part of their lives. Andrew Harvey writes the foreword to each volume, an insightful, personal introduction to each classic.

Bhagavad Gita: *Annotated & Explained*
Translation by *Shri Purohit Swami*; Annotation by *Kendra Crossen Burroughs*

"The very best Gita for first-time readers." —Ken Wilber

Millions of people turn daily to India's most beloved holy book, whose universal appeal has made it popular with non-Hindus and Hindus alike. This edition introduces you to the characters; explains references and philosophical terms; shares the interpretations of famous spiritual leaders and scholars; and more. 5½ x 8½, 192 pp, Quality PB, ISBN 1-893361-28-4 **$16.95**

The Way of a Pilgrim: *Annotated & Explained*
Translation and annotation by *Gleb Pokrovsky*

The classic of Russian spirituality—now with facing-page commentary that illuminates and explains the text for you.

This delightful account is the story of one man who sets out to learn the prayer of the heart—also known as the "Jesus prayer"—and how the practice transforms his existence. This edition guides you through an abridged version of the text with facing-page annotations explaining the names, terms and references. 5½ x 8½, 160 pp, Quality PB, ISBN 1-893361-31-4 **$14.95**

The Gospel of Thomas: *Annotated & Explained*
Translation and annotation by *Stevan Davies*

The recently discovered mystical sayings of Jesus—now with facing-page commentary that illuminates and explains the text for you.

Discovered in 1945, this collection of aphoristic sayings sheds new light on the origins of Christianity and the intriguing figure of Jesus, portraying the Kingdom of God as a present fact about the world, rather than a future promise or future threat. This edition guides you through the text with annotations that focus on the meaning of the sayings, ideal for readers with no previous background in Christian history or thought.
5½ x 8½, 192 pp, Quality PB, ISBN 1-893361-45-4 **$16.95**

SkyLight Illuminations Series
Andrew Harvey, series editor

Zohar: *Annotated & Explained*
Translation and annotation by *Daniel C. Matt*

The cornerstone text of Kabbalah.

The best-selling author of *The Essential Kabbalah* brings together in one place the most important teachings of the *Zohar*, the canonical text of Jewish mystical tradition. Guides you step by step through the midrash, mystical fantasy and Hebrew scripture that make up the *Zohar*, explaining the inner meanings in facing-page commentary. Ideal for readers without any prior knowledge of Jewish mysticism.

5½ x 8½, 176 pp, Quality PB, ISBN 1-893361-51-9 **$15.95**

Selections from the Gospel of Sri Ramakrishna
Annotated & Explained
Translation by *Swami Nikhilananda*; Annotation by *Kendra Crossen Burroughs*

The words of India's greatest example of God-consciousness and mystical ecstasy in recent history.

Introduces the fascinating world of the Indian mystic and the universal appeal of his message that has inspired millions of devotees for more than a century. Selections from the original text and insightful yet unobtrusive commentary highlight the most important and inspirational teachings. Ideal for readers without any prior knowledge of Hinduism.

5½ x 8½, 240 pp, b/w photographs, Quality PB, ISBN 1-893361-46-2 **$16.95**

 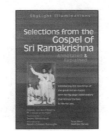  

Dhammapada: *Annotated & Explained*
Translation by *Max Müller* and revised by *Jack Maguire*; Annotation by *Jack Maguire*

The classic of Buddhist spiritual practice.

The Dhammapada—words spoken by the Buddha himself over 2,500 years ago—is notoriously difficult to understand for the first-time reader. Now you can experience it with understanding even if you have no previous knowledge of Buddhism. Enlightening facing-page commentary explains all the names, terms, and references, giving you deeper insight into the text.

5½ x 8½, 160 pp, Quality PB, ISBN 1-893361-42-X **$14.95**

Hasidic Tales: *Annotated & Explained*
Translation and annotation by *Rabbi Rami Shapiro*

The legendary tales of the impassioned Hasidic rabbis.

The allegorical quality of Hasidic tales can be perplexing. Here, they are presented as stories rather than parables, making them accessible and meaningful. Each demonstrates the spiritual power of unabashed joy, offers lessons for leading a holy life, and reminds us that the Divine can be found in the everyday. Annotations explain theological concepts, introduce major characters, and clarify references unfamiliar to most readers.

5½ x 8½, 192 pp, Quality PB, ISBN 1-893361-86-1 **$16.95**

Children's Spirituality

Ten Amazing People
And How They Changed the World
by *Maura D. Shaw*; Foreword by *Dr. Robert Coles*
Full-color illus. by *Stephen Marchesi*

For ages 6–10

Black Elk • Dorothy Day • Malcolm X • Mahatma Gandhi • Martin Luther King, Jr. • Mother Teresa • Janusz Korczak • Desmond Tutu • Thich Nhat Hanh • Albert Schweitzer

This vivid, inspirational, and authoritative book will open new possibilities for children by telling the stories of how ten of the past century's greatest leaders changed the world in important ways.

8½, x 11, 48 pp, HC, Full-color illus., ISBN 1-893361-47-0 **$17.95**

God's Paintbrush
by *Sandy Eisenberg Sasso*; Full-color illus. by *Annette Compton*

For ages 4 & up

Invites children of all faiths and backgrounds to encounter God openly in their own lives. Wonderfully interactive; provides questions adult and child can explore together at the end of each episode. "An excellent way to honor the imaginative breadth and depth of the spiritual life of the young." —Dr. Robert Coles, Harvard University

11 x 8½, 32 pp, HC, Full-color illus., ISBN 1-879045-22-2 **$16.95**

Also available:
A Teacher's Guide 8½ x 11, 32 pp, PB, ISBN 1-879045-57-5 **$8.95**
God's Paintbrush Celebration Kit 9½ x 12, HC, Includes 5 sessions/40 full-color Activity Sheets and Teacher Folder with complete instructions, ISBN 1-58023-050-4 **$21.95**

In God's Name
by *Sandy Eisenberg Sasso*; Full-color illus. by *Phoebe Stone*

For ages 4 & up

Like an ancient myth in its poetic text and vibrant illustrations, this award-winning modern fable about the search for God's name celebrates the diversity and, at the same time, the unity of all the people of the world. "What a lovely, healing book!" —Madeleine L'Engle

9 x 12, 32 pp, HC, Full-color illus., ISBN 1-879045-26-5 **$16.95**

Also available in Spanish:
El nombre de Dios 9 x 12, 32 pp, HC, Full-color illus., ISBN 1-893361-63-2 **$16.95**

Where Does God Live?
by *August Gold* and *Matthew J. Perlman*

For ages 3–6

Using simple, everyday examples that children can relate to, this colorful book helps young readers develop a personal understanding of God.

10 x 8½, 32 pp, Quality PB, Full-color photo illus., ISBN 1-893361-39-X **$8.95**

Religious Etiquette/Reference

How to Be a Perfect Stranger, 3rd Edition
The Essential Religious Etiquette Handbook
Edited by *Stuart M. Matlins* and *Arthur J. Magida*

The indispensable guidebook to help the well-meaning guest when visiting other people's religious ceremonies.

A straightforward guide to the rituals and celebrations of the major religions and denominations in the United States and Canada from the perspective of an interested guest of any other faith, based on information obtained from authorities of each religion. Belongs in every living room, library, and office.

COVERS:

African American Methodist Churches • Assemblies of God • Baha'i • Baptist • Buddhist • Christian Church (Disciples of Christ) • Christian Science (Church of Christ, Scientist) • Churches of Christ • Episcopalian and Anglican • Hindu • Islam • Jehovah's Witnesses • Jewish • Lutheran • Mennonite/Amish • Methodist • Mormon (Church of Jesus Christ of Latter-day Saints) • Native American/First Nations • Orthodox Churches • Pentecostal Church of God • Presbyterian • Quaker (Religious Society of Friends) • Reformed Church in America/Canada • Roman Catholic • Seventh-day Adventist • Sikh • Unitarian Universalist • United Church of Canada • United Church of Christ

6 x 9, 432 pp, Quality PB, ISBN 1-893361-67-5 **$19.95**

Also available:

The Perfect Stranger's Guide to Funerals and Grieving Practices
A Guide to Etiquette in Other People's Religious Ceremonies
Edited by *Stuart M. Matlins*
6 x 9, 240 pp, Quality PB, ISBN 1-893361-20-9 **$16.95**

The Perfect Stranger's Guide to Wedding Ceremonies
A Guide to Etiquette in Other People's Religious Ceremonies
Edited by *Stuart M. Matlins*
6 x 9, 208 pp, Quality PB, ISBN 1-893361-19-5 **$16.95**

Spirituality

Journeys of Simplicity
Traveling Light with Thomas Merton, Bashō, Edward Abbey, Annie Dillard & Others
by *Philip Harnden*

There is a more graceful way of traveling through life.

Offers vignettes of forty "travelers" and the few ordinary things they carried with them—from place to place, from day to day, from birth to death. What Thoreau took to Walden Pond. What Thomas Merton packed for his final trip to Asia. What Annie Dillard keeps in her writing tent. What an impoverished cook served M. F. K. Fisher for dinner. Much more.

"'How much should I carry with me?' is the quintessential question for any journey, especially the journey of life. Herein you'll find sage, sly, wonderfully subversive advice."
—Bill McKibben, author of *The End of Nature* and *Enough*
5 x 7¼, 128 pp, HC, ISBN 1-893361-76-4 **$16.95**

The Alphabet of Paradise
An A–Z of Spirituality for Everyday Life
by *Howard Cooper*

"An extraordinary book." —Karen Armstrong

One of the most eloquent new voices in spirituality, Howard Cooper takes us on a journey of discovery—into ourselves and into the past—to find the signposts that can help us live more meaningful lives. In twenty-six engaging chapters—from A to Z—Cooper spiritually illuminates the subjects of daily life, using an ancient Jewish mystical method of interpretation that reveals both the literal and more allusive meanings of each. Topics include: Awe, Bodies, Creativity, Dreams, Emotions, Sports, and more.
5 x 7¾, 224 pp, Quality PB, ISBN 1-893361-80-2 **$16.95**

Earth, Water, Fire, and Air
Essential Ways of Connecting to Spirit
by *Cait Johnson*

Spiritual nourishment at its most basic— the elemental approach to spirituality

You can't help but be drawn into the elemental approach to spirituality so gracefully detailed in this book. It identifies the four basic elements as humanity's first ways of knowing Spirit and reminds us of their value as keys to self-healing and re-connection. Offers a fascinating look at element-based symbols, traditions, and ceremonies, with creative activity suggestions for both individuals and groups.
6 x 9, 224 pp, Hardcover, ISBN 1-893361-65-9 **$19.95**